*Life
from the
Up Side*

Life from the Up Side

Seeing God at Work in the World

J. ELLSWORTH KALAS

DIMENSIONS
FOR LIVING
NASHVILLE

LIFE FROM THE UP SIDE
SEEING GOD AT WORK IN THE WORLD

Copyright © 2004 by Dimensions for Living

This book is printed on acid-free paper.

Library of Congress Cataloging-in-Publication Data

Kalas, J. Ellsworth, 1923-
  Life from the up side : seeing God at work in the world / J. Ellsworth Kalas.
    p. cm.
  ISBN 0-687-03730-1 (adhesive, pbk. : alk. paper)
  1. Consolation. I. Title.
  BV4905.3.K35 2004
  242—dc22

                                                    2003025778

04 05 06 07 08 09 10 11 12 13—10 9 8 7 6 5 4 3 2 1
MANUFACTURED IN THE UNITED STATES OF AMERICA

To
Wini Grizzle
and
Nellie Moser
For the privilege of working with you for nearly two decades and
for your commitment to holy excellence

CONTENTS

INTRODUCTION

I confess that I am an unreconstructed optimist. Not a *naive* one; I've lived too long for that, long enough to have experienced a resounding case for pessimism. I have vivid memories of the Great Depression, and I've lived through several wars and those international anomalies that we call police actions. I've watched what has seemed to me to be a rather steady decline in both public and private morals and a growing confusion about ethics. And of course, I've watched the increasing prevalence of both evil and inanity (sometimes they're synonymous) on television and the Internet.

But, there is God. And because there is God, there is goodness. I profoundly believe that God is at work in our world and that our planet has not yet been written off as a lost cause. History seems to tell me that though our human race appears so often to dedicate itself to its own destruction, God is always at work—usually, I think, behind the scenes. And because of God, faith, love, and goodness keep being reborn.

So I write about *Life from the Up Side.*

Some of you know me from earlier books, in which I've approached the wondrous material of the Old and New Testaments "from the Back Side." In a way, this book, too, is from the Back Side. It is, at any rate, if you ordinarily look at life through the general news of the day. The daily reports are of fire and flood, rape and pillage, and disasters both personal and general. Even the sports section is no longer much of an escape, now that drugs and strikes and obscene economics claim more sports lineage than batting averages and touchdowns. So if you get your view of life from the media's daily fare, then what I offer is from the Back Side— the *other* side, that is.

Because this book is concentrating on the wonderful, beautiful, hopeful side. Not naively; as I said earlier, I've lived too long for that. Nor am I suggesting a view that happiness will simply fall into our hands. The goodness that comes will be a cooperative venture in which you and I ally with God. But I am voting enthusiastically for the side of life that we see when we look at the Bible and at God. The *Up Side.*

J. Ellsworth Kalas

CHAPTER *1*

On Being Born with a Rusty Spoon
(For Those Who've Had a Bad Start)

JOSHUA 2:1-11: Then Joshua son of Nun sent two men secretly from Shittim as spies, saying, "Go, view the land, especially Jericho." So they went, and entered the house of a prostitute whose name was Rahab, and spent the night there. The king of Jericho was told, "Some Israelites have come here tonight to search out the land." Then the king of Jericho sent orders to Rahab, "Bring out the men who have come to you, who entered your house, for they have come only to search out the whole land." But the woman took the two men and hid them. Then she said, "True, the men came to me, but I did not know where they came from. And when it was time to close the gate at dark, the men went out. Where the men went I do not know. Pursue them quickly, for you can overtake them." She had, however, brought them up to the roof and

hidden them with the stalks of flax that she had laid out on the roof. So the men pursued them on the way to the Jordan as far as the fords. As soon as the pursuers had gone out, the gate was shut.

Before they went to sleep, she came up to them on the roof and said to the men: "I know that the LORD has given you the land, and that dread of you has fallen on us, and that all the inhabitants of the land melt in fear before you. For we have heard how the LORD dried up the water of the Red Sea before you when you came out of Egypt, and what you did to the two kings of the Amorites that were beyond the Jordan, to Sihon and Og, whom you utterly destroyed. As soon as we heard it, our hearts melted, and there was no courage left in any of us because of you. The LORD your God is indeed God in heaven above and on earth below.

11

*T*he most surprising thing about the phrase in my title for this chapter is that I've heard it only once. When I think of the number of people who have a right to say it, and those who express the same philosophy at greater length and with less eloquence, I'm surprised that this phrase hasn't become the possession of a whole subsection of our culture.

I got the phrase secondhand from a man who worked with my wife some years ago. It was one of those Monday morning conversations, when workers are sipping coffee and inquiring about the weekend just past. When someone asked if the others had had a good night's sleep, one man answered, "I never get a good night's sleep. I was born with a rusty spoon in my mouth."

As my wife, Janet, reports it, the statement wasn't bitter. The speaker was a pleasant man, not given to pessimism or complaint. He was making a summary of life as he had experienced it. The "rusty spoon" said it all.

When I heard the story, I said to myself, *Now, there's someone who knows his theology.* Of course, he's right—not just for himself, but for the whole human race. Mind you, the analysis is more pronounced and obvious in some cases, sometimes even to the level of consummate tragedy. But the man who said it, whether he knew it or not, was doing nothing other than putting the Christian doctrine of original sin in graphic, down-to-earth language. All of us were born with a rusty spoon. As for those to whom we sometimes enviously refer as having been born with a *silver* spoon in their mouths, if you'll look more carefully at their equipment, you'll find the silver is well tarnished. And you don't have to be a theologian to see it; a rudimentary knowledge of psychology will do. We don't start life with a spoon of our own making or choosing; it's been passed to us by other generations.

The classic doctrine of original sin says that when Adam and Eve sinned, they brought a curse upon the whole human race. In other words, they bequeathed to us a rusty spoon. Our Puritan ancestors taught this doctrine to their children as part of the alphabet. Since the issue is so basic, they were pretty pragmatic in doing so, especially since "A is for Adam": "In Adam's Fall, / We sinned all."

And that's the way it is. We know this not because we've read the doctrine but because we're human beings who have experienced it. We live every day with its reality.

Please understand me. I'm not speaking simply of our conduct. That's sometimes convincing enough when we find ourselves doing and saying things that we insist are inconsistent with our self-image. "I can't believe I did such a thing," we sometimes say as we review some irrational or unseemly act. Well, maybe it's an old family trait. Maybe it's something we learned from Adam and Eve.

But I repeat, I'm not speaking simply of our conduct. I'm thinking of all the other evidences that we are born into a world where sin was here before we were. Ponder our human scene. You didn't ask for a world where there's poverty, disease, and war; they were here waiting for you when you came. We inherited them. Let me hasten to add that we also didn't ask for a world where there are such things as the music of Bach, the writing of Shakespeare, and the art of Michelangelo; these, too, were waiting when we came. But in truth, all of us are born into a world where sin (as well as beauty) has a head start on us. It's a world where we are exposed early to pain, hatred, thoughtlessness, and irritability so that these unpleasant realities can easily become factors in our own personalities before we realize it. And this is true even before we get into the embarrassing business of those inclinations and traits that our families tell us we got from some relative who we wish hadn't contributed to our genetic line.

Some theologian a generation ago said that every human being is born with a pack on his or her back. That is, we come into this world with an accumulation from previous generations. We are likely to take the good for granted; our worst sin in that respect is that we don't use our good inheritance more effectively. But our problem, of course, is coping with the bad. What do we do with the pack on our back? How do we handle the rusty spoon?

Before I go further, let me say that some people seem clearly to come out worse in this matter than others. Some are born with poor health, some with what seem to be limited talents. Some folks begin life with a particularly unpleasant temperament, and with such a start, they generally find that those around them cooperate in giving their unpleasantness reason to prosper. I'm sad that many are born into homes where the financial resources are desperately limited, and some (far worse) are born into settings where they're not wanted or to parents who are poorly equipped to love them and to raise them with beauty. Some spoons, that is, are rustier than others.

And incidentally, we never really know for sure about another person's spoon. We don't know the complete history of even our closest friend or family member. In every human life there are interior lands that no one can fully explore, not even the most trusted friend or the most astute counselor. So no one knows for sure the nature of your spoon or mine. And to be honest, sometimes—depending on our moods—we may not evaluate our own spoon too accurately.

When it comes to rusty spoons, let me tell you a story. You'll find it in the book of Joshua, in the Old Testament. You may be surprised to learn that you'll find three brief sequels to the story in the New Testament. It's the story of a woman named Rahab, who lived long ago (*very* long ago!) in the city of Jericho.

Let me get right to the point. Rahab was a prostitute, operating a house of ill fame at the wall of Jericho. Some make themselves more comfortable with this story by sanitizing it a bit—suggesting that Rahab simply ran a hotel— but this sanitizing can't honestly be done, and people who read their Bibles seriously ought not to try. Rahab was a prostitute. We don't know how she came to follow that commerce of the body. Perhaps her parents lived outside the law, so it seemed perfectly natural to her to follow such a course. Or perhaps she was forced into what Rudyard Kipling called "the most ancient profession in the world." But most likely, I think, is this: She grew up in a culture where there was little sense of sin, or on the other hand, little sense of the sacredness of the body. Therefore, her work was probably seen simply as another way of making a living.

But there's no way to take the inherent sting from it. Her house, built right into the wall of the city, was appropriately located, for she was out at the edge of life. She saw most men at their worst—some of them brutal, many of them crude, all of them furtive. There had to be something profoundly distasteful in having men pursue you in private, then studiously avoid your eyes in public. Hers was a rusty spoon kind of world. She lived at the edge of life: on the edge of the law, on the edge of love, on the edge of hope.

Then one day she found herself hosting two foreigners, Israelites. She had heard about the people of Israel; after all, in her business, she was often the first to get gossip and privileged information. There had been wondrous tales (she could hardly know where fact slipped into fiction) of the way these Israelites had escaped from Egypt, survived a generation in the howling wilderness, and were now marching like a motley but surprisingly disciplined army toward Jericho and the adjoining cities. Rumor had it that the Lord God was with them and that they were invincible. No doubt many of the people of Jericho scoffed at the rumors ("Nothing to worry about when your city has walls like ours!"). Somehow, however, Rahab felt deep within that the rumors were true and that these people were in a march of destiny.

I suspect I should interrupt the story for a moment to answer a question that may well be in your mind: What were these Israelite spies doing in a place like Rahab's? To be honest, I don't know. To give it the nicest spin, perhaps

Rahab's was the only place one could get lodging. Or perhaps since these two men were involved in an illegal business, spying, they went to the site of an illegal business where no questions would be asked. And there's the worst scenario: Maybe these two men were taking advantage of being far from the people who knew them.

In any event, I marvel in this story, as I do in so many others, at the unflinching honesty of the Bible. The Bible seems never to gloss over the failings of its characters, nor to explain them. It gives us the unadorned facts, and it leaves the rest to us. And I marvel still more that God so often takes the rather messy stuff of our lives and manages to bring good from it. This doesn't excuse our messiness (read that *sin*), but it does remind us that God is not undone by our weakness, our stupidity, or our wickedness. Rather, God has a remarkable penchant for mixing grace with our basest ingredients until the will of heaven comes to pass.

But back to our two spies and Rahab. I suspect that she watched these men very carefully. Since they were spying out the land, their presence was soon noticed in the community. Jericho was a cosmopolitan center where strangers were a daily fact of life. But strangers who have no obvious business and who seem particularly attentive to too many details are going to arouse suspicion—particularly when it's known that a marauding band from Egypt is in the territory. The king of Jericho ordered Rahab to turn in the men. Instead, she hid them. More than that, she lied to protect them.

Then she helped them escape. But before she did, she told them why she had protected them. I know the Lord is with you, she explained, and that he is leading you to victory. Promise me one thing: When you conquer Jericho, as you surely will, you will spare my family and me. The two spies agreed. They gave her a crimson cord and asked that she hang it from her window so that when their troops destroyed Jericho, anyone in her house would be saved (see Joshua 2:12-21).

Everything went as planned. Israel conquered Jericho, and Rahab and her family were spared. In fact, Rahab and her family became part of the nation of Israel. How much of a part? Well, the rest of her story appears in the New Testament. We next read of her in the opening chapter of the Gospel of Matthew in a list of the ancestors of Jesus. She is one of a quite exclusive list; only four women are mentioned by name in the genealogy of our Lord, and she is one of them. Because, as it happened, she married into the tribe of Judah, from which the ancestors of Jesus came, and she was in the direct line.

Then we read of her again in the New Testament letters of Hebrews and James. Both writers hold her up as an example to be imitated, but for different virtues. The Letter to the Hebrews includes her in the select company of its faith Hall of Fame: "By faith Rahab the prostitute did not perish with those who were disobedient, because she had received the spies in peace" (Hebrews 11:31). By her place in this chapter she is identified as one of the great exemplars of faith, along with Moses, Abraham, Sarah, and Noah. That's pretty impressive company for someone born with a rusty spoon!

She receives, if possible, even greater acclaim in the Letter of James. This apostolic writer wants to show that faith without works is dead, so he proves his point by telling the story of Abraham. Then, as if to show that there's more than one example for his argument, James continues, "Likewise, was not Rahab the prostitute also justified by works when she welcomed the messengers and sent them out by another road?" (James 2:25).

That is, the New Testament writers saw Rahab, the Jericho harlot, as a prime example of someone who demonstrated both faith and works. Poor as her beginning must have been, troubled as probably were her early and middle years, she became an ancestor of our Lord Jesus Christ and a case history in godly living.

So what does a person do with life's rusty spoon? How do

you manage when there are branches in your family tree that you'd rather not mention or when you're not really sure you have a tree? There's an ancient story—originating in Russia, I believe—in which a man is falsely accused of a crime and sent to prison. After many years his innocence is proved, and he is released. But in his freedom, he is marked by great heaviness and darkness.

His neighbors urge him to resume a normal life; instead, he becomes a stranger and a recluse. One day, in response to an earnest encourager, he takes a bottle and a long piece of wire. He bends and bends the wire, forcing it into the bottle. Then he breaks the bottle, and lifts out the wire. "Now you are free," he says to the wire, "to resume your normal life." Yet still the wire remained bent. So it was, he said, for him. His life had been too bent, too misshapen, by the years in prison, with his burden of false accusations. He could never again be what he was before life forced him into its bottle of shame and misery.

I empathize. There's no doubt that the circumstances and experiences of our lives mark and shape us, sometimes to the point of distortion. Some of us are twisted into all sorts of unhappy postures by a variety of factors—perhaps our parents, maybe a thoughtless teacher, unwholesome friendships, bad job experiences, or simply the ugly temperament we seem to have inherited and can't seem to control. Is one doomed, then, to remain so twisted?

The Bible gives a resounding answer, and Rahab demonstrates it as well as anyone. Whatever our circumstances, our start in life, or our present state of life, we can go on to something better. We will need *faith,* as Rahab did, and we also will have to *work* at it, as she did. But we *can* go on. I believe that no one can ever fully estimate how magnificently we can do so.

And consider this: In the case of Rahab, it was the very unseemliness of her situation that provided the opportunity for her to make the new start that led eventually to her unique role in history. After all, the spies would never have met Rahab if she had been one of the comfortable people in the Jericho community.

For the sixteen years that I was the senior minister at the Church of the Saviour in Cleveland, Ohio, I was inspired again and again by the beauty of the stained glass windows in the towering Gothic sanctuary. In time, I came upon a rusty spoon story. R. Toland Wright was the youngest child in a large family. His mother died when he was quite small. When his father remarried, the stepmother was a good woman, but a painfully practical one. She believed that artists were simply lazy people, so she wouldn't allow Toland to have any crayons or paper when he was a boy. As he grew older, she urged him to become a plumber because plumbing meant a steady income.

But the boy had a stubborn streak. When he was still quite young, he left home and got all kinds of odd jobs to earn his way through the art academy. Gradually his remarkable talents began to develop. In the height of his career, he created numbers of magnificent stained glass windows, including the chancel window and the baptistry window at the Church of the Saviour. Toland Wright had a rusty spoon: half-orphaned as a small child, deprived of the tools of art he so passionately desired, twisted like wire into a bottle of practicality—and yet he had faith in his sense of purpose, and he worked to make his faith come to pass.

I have no way of knowing where you are. If we were in a conversation, you might answer wryly, "Not where I'd *like* to be, that's for sure; not as good a human being, not as intelligent, not as effective in life or work." I understand. Neither am I.

But I encourage myself with the words of Helen Wodehouse. We so often think, she said, that the promise of God is, " 'At the end of the end of the way you may find me.' " Not so, she continues. God says, " 'I *am* the Way; I am the road under your feet, the road that begins just as low down as you happen to be.' If we are in a hole the Way begins in the hole" (Dorothy Berkley Phillips, ed., *The Choice Is Always Ours: An Anthology on the Religious Way* [Wheaton, Ill.: Re-Quest Books, 1975], p. 79).

Yes and Amen! So this is where we begin, right here, right now, in this place, this moment. Whatever our rusty spoon, let us use it well. Like Rahab, with faith and work we can accomplish the purposes of the Lord God, the purposes of grandeur that are potential in even the rustiest of spoons.

CHAPTER 2

When Life Is at January
(Who Knows What Wonders Lie Ahead?)

GENESIS 11:26-32: When Terah had lived seventy years, he became the father of Abram, Nahor, and Haran.

Now these are the descendants of Terah. Terah was the father of Abram, Nahor, and Haran; and Haran was the father of Lot. Haran died before his father Terah in the land of his birth, in Ur of the Chaldeans. Abram and Nahor took wives; the name of Abram's wife was Sarai, and the name of Nahor's wife was Milcah. She was the daughter of Haran the father of Milcah and Iscah. Now Sarai was barren; she had no child.

Terah took his son Abram and his grandson Lot son of Haran, and his daughter-in-law Sarai, his son Abram's wife, and they went out together from Ur of the Chaldeans to go into the land of Canaan; but when they came to Haran, they settled there. The days of Terah were two hundred five years; and Terah died in Haran.

*O*ne of the problems with life is that it's disorganized. I'm not speaking of your desk or your closet, or mine; discussing that might require more than one chapter. I'm speaking about life as a whole; it doesn't come to us organized. We have nothing to say about when our lives will start, nor usually about when they will end. Nor do we decide who our natural parents will be, what bloodline we'll have, where we'll be born, or under what circumstances.

Perhaps that's one reason sports appeal to us. They're organized, and they begin when we decide they should begin. A race begins when the gun is sounded, the basketball game when the referee throws the ball for the center jump, the baseball game when the umpire says, "Play ball!" That's neat and tidy, and we wish life could be that way. But life isn't; our lives started without our having anything to say about it. As a matter of fact, we don't even remember what happened—and perhaps that's a mercy, because birth itself must be very traumatic. So the ball game is already in progress when we arrive, and the race has already begun. We simply fit in as best we can.

In a sense (a quite peculiar sense), the book of Genesis describes creation in somewhat similar fashion. After the majestic opening sentence, "In the beginning God created the heaven and the earth," comes a surprising next line: "And the earth was without form, and void" (Genesis 1:1-2*a* KJV). It's almost as if the Bible were saying that God had a mess to begin with. A formless void and darkness, a surging, rolling mass of no discernible purpose, immersed in darkness. If we read with a sense of humor, we might think the writer of Genesis is inviting us to imagine God saying, "Now what can I do with a mess like this?" And it's almost as if the Bible were gently warning us, from the most profound of examples, that beginnings are almost never easy. This is because most of the time, we don't get to choose our beginnings; we're thrust into them.

What shall we say for a child born last night in some warravaged country where freedom is unknown? Or what shall we say for a baby born this morning to a crack-addicted mother in the most tragedy-ridden section of a metropolitan inner city? Or, on the other hand, what shall we say for a baby born to a lovely, prosperous suburban couple but who seems to have a kind of recessive gene that picks up all the moody, resentful, unpleasant characteristics from both sides of the family? We'll say that we don't get to begin this ball game the way we'd like to, in sensible, orderly fashion.

We're thrown into it, with the game, the race, already in progress.

And of course that's the trouble with January—January, that is, as we know it in the Northern Hemisphere. I remember when a grade school teacher, a very long time ago, told us about January. She said it was named for Janus, the mythological Roman god of doorways, because Janus had two faces, one looking forward and one looking backward, just as the first month of the year does. Well, I've lived through scores of Januarys in Iowa, Wisconsin, and Cleveland, Ohio, and I've concluded that Janus looked both ways because he didn't want to look at the present—at the cold, the drizzly rain, the snow, and the slush.

I don't know that anyone has ever said it better than that remarkable woman Jane Hess Merchant. She put it in a poem some years ago in which she asked what good a person might expect from a year that starts with January (as all of them seem to do). She listed the usual problems many of us associate with January: heating bills, post-Christmas blues, bitter winds, frozen streets, and a variety of viruses.

Then she reminds us that a year must start somewhere, and that perhaps part of January's worth is that it forces us, by its very nature, to new resolves when we need them most. Miss Merchant concludes, "And all my life I have discovered very / Good things in years that start with January!" (Jane Merchant, *Because It's Here,* [Nashville: Abingdon Press, 1970], p. 54).

That makes me want to tell you a story. I think of it as a January kind of story, and I think in time you'll understand what I mean. It comes from a bad season; that is, a bad moral, ethical, and spiritual season. The world had become such a mess that God had dealt an extreme remedy, a devastating flood, as an attempt to purge creation and give it a new start (see Genesis 6:11–9:17). But in a surprisingly short time after that new start, human beings again had messed things up, and the next thing you know, they were building a tower in Babel in a further absurd act of defiance against

God. And as a result, they were now in more trouble than ever. It was trouble that had come because they couldn't understand one another, couldn't *communicate,* to use a modern phrase (see Genesis 11:1-9).

So when the book of Genesis has finished telling us the dreary story of Babel, it begins listing the descendants of Shem. Ordinarily I don't get enthusiastic about a biblical genealogy, but it comes as a bit of a relief in this story, after coping with the Flood and the tower of Babel. After all, surely we can't get into any more trouble as long as we're simply being told that Shem was a hundred years old when he became the father of Arpachshad and lived five hundred years beyond this, while having other sons and daughters. As I said, considering the previous circumstances, this genealogy comes almost as a relief.

But, much like January itself, it just doesn't seem to be *going* anywhere! Then we read, "When Terah had lived seventy years, he became the father of Abram, Nahor, and Haran" (Genesis 11:26). *So what,* and *who cares?* Then the going-nowhere story says that Haran was the father of Lot, but Haran, unfortunately, died before his father did (Genesis 11:27-28). That's a sad notation, a kind of gesture of futility, because children ought not to die before their parents. The story continues with details that don't mean much, unless you know the rest of the story. And even then, you ask yourself about some of the details. You learn that Abram and Nahor took wives, and that the name of Abram's wife was Sarai, and the name of Nahor's wife was Milcah (Genesis 11:29).

The Bible is sparing of words. After all, the writers weren't working with a computer and an endless supply of paper. Every word had to be etched out on some difficult-to-obtain-and-prepare writing material, so they didn't waste words. But after mentioning Sarai and Milcah, the writer goes on to say, "Now Sarai was barren; she had no child" (Genesis 11:30).

That little sentence, that the writer emphasizes by giving

us the same information twice, in only slightly different language (she "was barren; she had no child") is meant either to reflect on Sarai or to prepare us for something very special—perhaps even a miracle. In that ancient world, having children was holy business. It really didn't matter what your religion was, whether pagan or divine, it was commonly felt that if you had a child, you were blessed by God or the gods, and if you didn't have a child, something was wrong—not with nature or the calendar, but in your relationship with the divine. If God approved of you, you had children; if you didn't have children, it must be that God, for whatever reason, didn't like you. So when the writer tells us that Sarai is barren and has no children, he is all but inviting us to ask, "What was wrong with her?"

The writer continues by reporting that Terah took his son Abram and his grandson Lot and his daughter-in-law Sarai and left the wonderful, progressive city of Ur in order to go to the land of Canaan. Obviously Terah has something in mind. The Bible doesn't tell us why Terah wanted to go to Canaan; in truth, Ur was a much nicer place to be. But whatever it was that impelled Terah to head to Canaan, he didn't make it. When the group got to Haran, "they settled there" (Genesis 11:31). So there you have two mysteries: why Terah ever thought of going to Canaan, and why he gave up the idea. And then, we are told, Terah died there. Sounds like the end of the story, and not a very impressive story at that.

But that, I tell you, is January! You say you don't like it? I don't blame you. Here is a little extended family that has chosen to leave one of the major centers of ancient civilization, Ur, in order to go to Canaan. It isn't an especially notable company because the only woman who is mentioned is a woman who can't have children. Then, they quit without reaching their destination, settling for Haran, and in Haran, the patriarch of the family dies.

But I have to tell you that this is the beginning of something *big*. As a matter of fact, it's the beginning of the biggest story in the history of our human race, because the next thing you read is something like this: Now the Lord said to Abram, Pick up on that trip that you interrupted a while ago, because I'm going to bless you, and make you a great nation, so that "in you all the families of the earth shall be blessed" (Genesis 12:3).

Who would have thought it? Who would have guessed when you were reading the dreary story of another human failure at Babel, a list of the descendants of Shem, and the particulars of a family that decided to leave civilization to venture into the unknown,only to give up partway there, that this is the beginning of the biggest story in the human race, especially considering that the woman of the family seems to be outside the blessing of heaven because she has no children?

Because, you see, from Abram (or Abraham, as he will later be called) will come the Jewish people. And from the Jewish people will come Jesus Christ. And from Jesus Christ will come the salvation of our human race for all who will accept him.

That's a January kind of story. It doesn't begin neat and tidy, as when a referee throws a ball into the air or when an umpire calls, "Play ball!" It begins with a human race that seems always to be messing things up, and with an extended family that starts on a long trip, then stops, and with a woman who can't have children. That's January stuff: viruses, and bills, and extra heating expenses, and sometimes slippery roads. After all, What good can a person expect in a year that begins with January?

Well, Jane Hess Merchant was a good one to raise the question and a great one to answer it. From the externals of her life, all of her days were a January. She was born with *osteogenesis imperfecta*, brittle bone disease. She was confined to a bed from the time she was twelve years old. She went for years at a time without leaving her home, because she had to be transported on a stretcher. By the time she was twenty-three, Jane was completely deaf and could communicate with others only by writing messages back and forth on a child's toy, a "magic slate." By the time she was thirty, she was nearly blind. But she said that what made life worth living for her was the knowledge that "to live is Christ." More than two thousand of her poems were published—most of them *humorous* poems! So when she wrote, "all my life I have discovered very / Good things in years that start with January," she spoke with authority.

Is the world without form, and void? Then expect that at any time the Spirit of God may blow over the face of the darkness and the void. Life isn't orderly and organized. No one says, "Play ball," so that you can start with the score nothing to nothing or with a clean slate. When you are born, the game has already begun, and the score may already be against you; in fact, it may already be *twenty to nothing* against you!

No matter! *That's* where you begin. "I wish," we say, "I wish we were already in Canaan land. I wish Sarai had a baby. I wish everybody loved me, and that I had an 'A' in geometry, and that our mortgage was paid, and that our children were all brilliant. But instead, here we are with Babel in the background and no sign of Canaan."

And God answers, "Now we have the devil just where we want him. It's January, and anything can happen." Because, you see, when we someday get to the place where we see "the holy city, the new Jerusalem, coming down out of heaven from God" (Revelation 21:2), we must remember that the story begins, in a historical sense, when an extended family leaves Ur of the Chaldeans with a woman named Sarai who can't have children. It's January, and who can say what God is going to do next?

CHAPTER 3

A Woman Who Lived with Scorn (For Those Who Suffer Rejection Close at Hand)

GENESIS 29:15-32: Then Laban said to Jacob, "Because you are my kinsman, should you therefore serve me for nothing? Tell me, what shall your wages be?" Now Laban had two daughters; the name of the elder was Leah, and the name of the younger was Rachel. Leah's eyes were lovely, and Rachel was graceful and beautiful. Jacob loved Rachel; so he said, "I will serve you seven years for your younger daughter Rachel." Laban said, "It is better that I give her to you than that I should give her to any other man; stay with me." So Jacob served seven years for Rachel, and they seemed to him but a few days because of the love he had for her.

Then Jacob said to Laban, "Give me my wife that I may go in to her, for my time is completed." So Laban gathered together all the people of the place, and made a feast. But in the evening he took his daughter Leah and brought her to Jacob; and he went in to her. (Laban gave his maid Zilpah to his daughter Leah to be her maid.) When morning came, it was Leah! And Jacob said to Laban, "What is this you have done to me? Did I not serve with you for Rachel? Why then have you deceived me?" Laban said, "This is not done in our country— giving the younger before the firstborn. Complete the week of this one, and we will give you the other also in return for serving me another seven years." Jacob did so, and completed her week; then Laban gave him his daughter Rachel as a wife. (Laban gave his maid Bilhah to his daughter Rachel to be her maid.) So Jacob went in to Rachel also, and he loved Rachel more than Leah. He served Laban for another seven years.

When the LORD saw that Leah was unloved, he opened her womb; but Rachel was bar-

ren. Leah conceived and bore a son, and she named him Reuben; for she said, "Because the LORD has looked on my affliction; surely now my husband will love me."

*P*erhaps in the total picture of life, a balance is struck. My belief in basic fairness insists that this must be so, or at least I pray that it is so. But along the way, a given member of a family, and sometimes an entire family, can justifiably feel that there's no equality or rightness in the way nature distributes its favors.

Several thousand years ago a certain wealthy farmer—Laban, by name—had two daughters. The older girl, Leah, was a fine person. Say it again, and underline it: Leah was a *fine* person. And she was gritty enough to hold out over the years; good for the long haul, one might say. But in the family beauty contest, she ran a poor showing. This is bad news, because in life as many experience it, family beauty contests are more important than those they run in places like Atlantic City.

You get the report on Leah in succinct form. The New Revised Standard Version says, "Leah's eyes were lovely" (Genesis 29:17), but it adds a footnote regarding "lovely": "Meaning of Hebrew uncertain." In truth, the NRSV seems to be a minority report; the other judges are not so kind. Everett Fox says that Leah's eyes were "delicate" (*The Five Books of Moses* [New York: Schocken Books, 1995], p. 137). The King James Version calls her "tender eyed." Both the New English Bible and the Revised English Bible say that Leah was "dull-eyed." I suspect that if Leah were left to herself without being cast in an unfair competition, she made a quite favorable impression. "A lovely girl," the neighbors probably said. "Yes, indeed, a fine girl. She'll make some man a good wife."

One thing was wrong: She had a younger sister. If it hadn't been for the younger sister, I think Leah would have been well received, even within the worst description of her eyes. But beside her younger sister, Leah faded back into the scenery, as if her only purpose in life were to serve as a setting and backdrop for the glamorous Rachel.

E. A. Speiser's translation of Genesis describes the situation in this simple, straightforward way: "Leah had tender eyes, but Rachel was shapely and beautiful" (*Anchor Bible* [New York, Doubleday, 1964], p. 224). There you have it. When Leah walked into a gathering, people responded pleasantly, even ecstatically, but when Rachel came along, they forgot that Leah was present. All eyes, inevitably, fastened on Rachel. If she frowned, the room grew quiet; if she laughed, the room became merry. When she walked out of the room, every eye—especially every male eye—followed her, admiring, perhaps even adoring her. This was the emotional setting in which Leah became an eligible young woman.

Then one day a young man appeared on the scene, unexpectedly and dramatically, as in an old-fashioned movie. He had ties with their father's side of the family and was an especially suitable marriage candidate. But unfortunately for Leah, the young man—Jacob—saw Rachel first, and promptly fell in love (see Genesis 29:1-14). We could call it "love at first sight," and I'll venture that it wasn't the first time someone was so smitten with Rachel.

When Jacob had visited and worked for Rachel's and Leah's father for a month, Laban asked what salary he would like. Jacob answered, "The hand of Rachel in marriage." Laban thought this was a good idea. He suggested that Jacob work seven years, and then he could marry Rachel. The Bible says that those seven years seemed to Jacob but a few days because of the love he had for Rachel. I *told* you she was that kind of person! Exciting, if she isn't your competitor.

When the seven-year term was complete, Jacob asked for

his wife. Laban brought together all the people of the area for a feast. Then, in the dark of the evening, he put his older daughter, Leah, in the marriage tent. It was the custom in that culture to bring the bride to the chamber heavily veiled. Early rabbinical scholars add to the plot: They speculated that Rachel and Leah were twins, with Leah being the older of the two. Whatever was the case, in the darkness of the marriage night, Jacob claimed Leah for his wife. In the light of the next morning, Jacob discovered the deception Laban had worked on him. When he complained to his father-in-law, Laban replied that in their culture, the older daughter must be married first and that after the week of marriage festivities was ended, he could also marry Rachel, if he would be willing to work another seven years for her. Jacob, angered but perhaps more anxious than ever to have Rachel, agreed to the hard bargain.

I think we have to recognize that Leah had cooperated with her father's scheme; after all, she helped deceive Jacob on that wedding night. Perhaps some would blame her for that. But don't be hard on her. In that ancient world, I'm sure she had little choice. Her father's word was law, and when he ordered her to take her sister's place, veiled, in the marriage tent, and to leave Jacob with the impression she was Rachel, she was compelled to do so.

And I'm sure something else was going on. Almost certainly, Leah must have entertained a dream: *If only I am given a chance, Jacob will be pleased with me and will come someday to love me.* I don't chide her for such a dream. Many a person has taken a job just out of reach, entered a relationship of doubtful prospects, engaged in a hopeless pursuit in the expectation that somehow it will work, no matter how much the odds are against it.

Instead, Leah became a woman who lived with scorn. At first the writer of Genesis says simply that Jacob "loved Rachel more than Leah" (Genesis 29:30), and that's bad enough. But after the passage of a few years and the birth of her second son, Leah said, "The LORD has heard that I am hated" (Genesis 29:33). A tough-minded observer might say that Leah brought it on herself. In a strained world of two women and one man, did Jacob treat her with indifference while he sought out Rachel in devotion and passion? Did he ignore Leah, hardly knowing she was part of his life, except for those times when Rachel was unavailable? I think Leah tried, at first, to make each such occasion count, hoping she could at last, one way or another, gain Jacob's love.

And who knows. Perhaps for a time her efforts succeeded in some measure. But when you know that another is loved while you are only endured and you are greeted indifferently while the other person is embraced and sought out, well, eventually you begin to lose heart. What little confidence you have (especially if you are considered "dull-eyed") drains away. When you have a chance to speak, you say the wrong thing. When an opportunity presents itself, you stumble over it. Then, in self-defense, you become resentful and bitter and caustic so that you, yourself, destroy whatever small talent you had for success. Your defeat begins to feed on itself. Knowing that you are not wanted, you at first become unsure of yourself, then you become pathetic, and at last, perhaps, hateful.

How many in our world have to live with scorn? Scorn is an equal opportunity demon, as ready to attack rich as poor, young as old, male as female; scorn has no preference for one race over another, though some races have encountered scorn more often over the centuries. Nor can we ever reach some place in life where we are exempt from scorn. The powerful can buy or control certain favors, but outside the realm of their influence, they are as subject to scorn as the most abject soul.

Scorn is at its worst in the more intimate relationships of life, especially within family, social circle, or neighborhood. And what does it do to a person to live with scorn day in, day out? What happens inside, *deep* inside? I seem to recall a vignette in a Thomas Wolfe novel. A strong, aggressive wife begins an affair. She makes no secret of it from her quiet, rather weak husband. Each evening her lover, a burly man, stops by to pick her up for their rendezvous, while the husband looks on helplessly. But one night the husband rises up tentatively to protest, and when he does, the lover throws him to the ground like a rag, beating and humiliating him. Every night thereafter, the beaten husband stands watering his lawn, his eyes downcast, while his wife and her lover drive off with peals of laughter. What happens to a human being who lives with such scorn?

In your childhood, was there a girl who seemed always to be alone on the edge of the playground or a boy who was slower than the rest so that some snickered behind their hands each time he was called on to recite? Was there a student who seemed to have no saving grace of attractiveness so that he or she always walked home alone? Or what of the child who is told again and again by insensitive or harried parents that he or she is stupid, or plain, or lacking in social grace? Do you know a spouse who feels that home itself is alien territory and whose only value seems to be in providing resources or care for others?

Do we know how many people live with scorn, how many hurt inside, *deep* inside? The newspeople and the feature writers tell us that we live in a violent age, a time when people destroy with shotgun blasts. And it is a violent age, of course; we see it day after day. But perhaps just as bad, and far more prevalent, is the style of sophisticated violence that shows itself on all sides, as people use a demonic variety of psychological devices to belittle and deteriorate human personality. They would never shoot another person; blood would repulse them. But they delight in goading with words, or a knowing glance; or perhaps simply by so obviously excluding. Jesus made the point clear: The person who says to another, "You fool!" is in as much danger of hell fire as the one who murders (Matthew 5:21-22).

What happens to a body of people, a whole race or ethnic group, who live with rejection and scorn? Langston Hughes, the African American poet, asked, "What happens to a dream deferred?" It can dry up, "like a raisin in the sun," but it's also possible that it can "fester like a sore"; or worse, it can even "explode" ("Harlem," 1951).

What about the underemployed or the constantly unemployed, the unsophisticated, the physically unattractive, the always poor? What happens to humans who live with scorn? Some become permanently beaten; they decide that their place in life is a place of defeat; that they have so little to offer that they'd do better to withdraw from life's scene. I wonder how many contributions to human welfare have never been given because some person lost heart because of constant rejection. Some who live with scorn build a defensive shell; we see them as bitter or hateful, and if they are so, they then pour still more scorn into the stream of daily living. A spouse who feels scorned can easily become overly possessive of children until sometimes the children become pawns in the domestic game; or in other instances, someone made to feel inferior at work becomes unjustly critical at work or in the circle of friendship.

But back to the story of Leah, a woman who lived with scorn. Night after night, week after week, she lived on life's emotional leftovers, played second fiddle. And then, the writer of Genesis says, God intervened. "When the LORD saw that Leah was unloved, he opened her womb; but Rachel was barren" (Genesis 29:31). In that ancient world, nothing was so important for a woman as that she should bear children. In the years that followed, Leah had four sons, then two more, and later still, a daughter.

And in the long reach of the story, that isn't all. One of Leah's sons was Judah. And from the descendants of Judah came Israel's greatest king, David, and a whole line of rulers. And there's still more. When the New Testament unfolds the continuing story of God's work in our world, it reveals that it is from Leah's son Judah that our Lord Jesus Christ has come. So much of the latter portion of the book of Genesis is dedicated to the story of Joseph, a son of Rachel, but the grand plot of the Scriptures takes its course through Judah, Leah's son.

There's also a peculiar personal twist to Leah's story. She was preceded in death by her sister, Rachel, who died in childbirth when her second son, Benjamin, was born, and Rachel was buried "on the way to Ephrath" (Genesis 35:19). Leah's death came somewhat later; and when Jacob was dying, he asked to be buried near Mamre, in the field where his grandparents, Abraham and Sarah, and his parents, Isaac and Rebekah, were buried; and Jacob adds, "and there I buried Leah" (Genesis 49:31).

I'm not suggesting that the pain of Leah's rejection was relieved by being buried next to her husband, removed from her sister Rachel, nor by the glory that came long after her death in the kingship of David and the coming of Jesus, the Messiah. Mind you, I think Leah's place in genealogical history is enviable, but unless she possessed some great faith that is not referred to in the Scriptures, I can't feel that she found any succor in the prospect that she might someday be made famous, or at least be legitimized, by her descendants. One needs remarkable inner toughness to be able to say, in days of scorn, "Someday you will have to respect me." Perhaps Leah had such inner toughness. I see some such toughness, surely, in the tenacity with which she held to Jacob. But I can't honestly find elements of comfort in her story.

But several lessons are to be learned. For those who live with scorn, whether only occasionally or through most of their lives, I offer no casual bromides. Pain is pain, and as far as psychic pain is concerned, scorn is one of the most debilitating. But the Scriptures are clear. God has a particular prejudice for those who are oppressed and at a disadvantage. God is never blind to human injustice, and God's heart is never insensitive to human hurt.

And for those who will let it be so, there is remarkable satisfaction in the stuff of the struggle. As surely as some people follow a particular vocational course because they find its danger exhilarating or its difficulties ego-building, I believe some people come to take pride in the way they've managed to cope with a bad scene. I'm very sure Leah developed a remarkable inner toughness. If you had known her in her old age, you might well have found a woman of composure, strength, and a quiet sense of victory.

Let me add a special word for those of us who feel that, as Christians, we should show something of God's concern for those who live, or have lived, with scorn. Is there anything we can do to express the concern that rests in the heart of God? We can begin by examining our lives, to see what individuals, or what groups or races, we are perhaps treating indifferently or with scorn. Are there such persons within our circle of life: a student in the school where we teach, a clerk in the store where we shop, a neighbor on the street where we live—persons who live with scorn, and who are slowly being broken by it? If we can identify any such person or group, we should feel compelled to extend every possible act of human kindness, in the hope that we might mitigate the pain of scorn with which such persons live.

Ancient Leah was buried long ago in Mamre, but her spiritual descendants are everywhere. Some days you may count yourself among them; most of us have such occasions. But some folks spend most of life, perhaps all of life, broken by scorn. We must become sensitive enough to see these Leahs, to care, and to help. This we must do for those who live with scorn.

CHAPTER 4

Don't Blame the Donkey!
(Capitalize on Your Adversity)

NUMBERS 22:21-34: So Balaam got up in the morning, saddled his donkey, and went with the officials of Moab.

God's anger was kindled because he was going, and the angel of the LORD took his stand in the road as his adversary. Now he was riding on the donkey, and his two servants were with him. The donkey saw the angel of the LORD standing in the road, with a drawn sword in his hand; so the donkey turned off the road, and went into the field; and Balaam struck the donkey, to turn it back onto the road. Then the angel of the LORD stood in a narrow path between the vineyards, with a wall on either side. When the donkey saw the angel of the LORD, it scraped against the wall, and scraped Balaam's foot against the wall; so he struck it again. Then the angel of the LORD went ahead, and stood in a narrow place, where there was no way to turn either to the right or to the left. When the donkey saw the angel of the LORD, it lay down under Balaam; and Balaam's anger was kindled, and he struck the donkey with his staff. Then the LORD opened the mouth of the donkey, and it said to Balaam, "What have I done to you, that you have struck me these three times?" Balaam said to the donkey, "Because you have made a fool of me! I wish I had a sword in my hand! I would kill you right now!" But the donkey said to Balaam, "Am I not your donkey, which you have ridden all your life to this day? Have I been in the habit of treating you this way?" And he said, "No."

Then the LORD opened the eyes of Balaam, and he saw the angel of the LORD standing in the road, with his drawn sword in his hand; and he bowed down, falling on his face. The angel of the LORD said to him, "Why have you struck your donkey these three times? I have come out as an adversary, because your way is perverse before me. The donkey saw me, and turned away from me these three times. If it had not turned away from me, surely just now I would have killed you and let it live." Then Balaam said to the angel of the LORD, "I have sinned, for I did not know that you were standing in the road to oppose me. Now therefore, if it is displeasing to you, I will return home."

We say a lot about the merits and the shortcomings of the School of Experience. As I view it, the biggest problem in this school is our failure to recognize the faculty when they come to teach us. We're a dull lot, you and I. The teacher strides into the room, takes the tutorial spot at the podium, and asks for our attention. We leave our notebooks idle and our minds closed! Sometimes the teacher then goes to sublime lengths; very little of the teaching in the School of Experience is by lecture, you know. If it were, we might at least recognize when we were into a lesson. But Experience does its work mainly by example, by "for instances," by laboratory experiments. Isn't that what we mean by School of Experience? It's learning by *experiment*, by the stuff of the laboratory. Unfortunately, these experiments are not idle practice; they *count*. Sometimes, like a novice in a chemistry class, we put together some formula that explodes in our face, making trouble for those around us as well as for ourselves. That's what we mean by "a costly experience."

But the issue is that we don't always recognize our teachers. Sometimes we don't even realize we're in school. It is no wonder, then, that we're slow to learn.

Many centuries ago there was a man so wise that his name is recorded for us still today, both in the Scriptures and in some secular writings of ancient times. His name was Balaam.

It was said that he had the power to put curses on people and even on cities or nations, or, on the other hand, to pronounce blessings on them. So people hired him to speak his blessing or his curse. I suspect that sometimes those blessings were simply his counsel. Part of his wisdom, of course, is that he knew when to say yes or no to the requests that came for his services. His power apparently was widely recognized, so he had no business using it indiscriminately.

Balaam finds his way into our Bible because one day a king, Balak of Moab, tried to enlist his services to curse the nation of Israel (see Numbers 22:1-21). When this wise man, Balaam, discussed the project with God, he immediately was told to reject the offer. The nation Israel was the apple of God's eye, and Balaam was told to avoid any negative business with her.

But wise as Balaam was, he nevertheless had an appetite for worldly goods and for prestige. Every wise person has a blind spot, and for many it's a place involving wealth, prestige, or both. So when King Balak came back with a better offer, delivered by an even more impressive delegation, Balaam decided to think it over. Furthermore, he tipped his hand. When the delegation said that the king would reward him handsomely, Balaam replied, "Even if he gave me his palace filled with silver and gold, I could not do what he's asking." Well, when people tell you how large a price they're ready to resist, they've also told you in what area you should do your bidding.

So Balaam asked for time to think over the offer. In a series of peculiar experiences, he decided to accompany the delegation, to see if perhaps he might curse Israel after all—even though God had warned him not to. That meant Balaam had to travel by the major mode of ancient transportation, a donkey. Still today, in many places of the world, the donkey remains a significant means of getting from one place to another and for effective transportation of goods. Fortunately, Balaam had a good donkey. It was one that had served him for years, faithfully and admirably.

But on this journey, the donkey began to act like, well, like a donkey, or what we popularly think of as a donkey's style. But not for the usual reasons. This donkey, as it happened, was smarter than his master. Of course, this is not entirely unprecedented; most of us have observed some instances where a "dumb" animal has exceeded the performed intelligence of its master.

Anyway, as they traveled to meet King Balak, the donkey suddenly saw something that Balaam and his entourage did not see: an angel in the middle of the road. So the donkey did what any intelligent donkey would do: It walked out into the field to avoid the obstruction. This seemed especially wise since the angel was standing with a drawn sword. Balaam, in his ignorance, beat the donkey to get it back onto the road.

A little farther down the road, the path led between two vineyards, and the angel appeared again. This time, as the donkey tried to avoid the angel, it crushed Balaam's foot against a vineyard wall. He beat the animal again. Then the angel of the Lord relocated to a place so narrow that there was no room to turn or to maneuver, "either to the right or to the left." So the donkey lay down. What else could it do? Now Balaam was angrier than ever, and he beat the donkey again. And no doubt this beating was more emphatic as befit Balaam's increasing anger.

The Bible tells us that at this point, the Lord opened the donkey's mouth. "What have I done to you," the donkey asked, "that you have struck me these three times?" (Numbers 22:28). Balaam's answer revealed a great deal about himself; far more, I'm sure, than he intended to reveal. "You have made a fool of me!" Balaam answered. Then he went on to say that if he had had a sword with him, he would have killed the donkey.

Let me observe that you can get the measure of a human being by discovering who or what can make a fool of the person. If a donkey can make a fool of you, you're obviously in big trouble. When you see a person making a fool of himself or herself over some minor matter—some poor donkey of a problem or a situation—you know a good deal about how big (or small) that person may be. Before you say, "So-and-so made a fool of me," ask yourself how big a person you're declaring yourself to be. If a donkey or its equivalent can do so, may the Lord have mercy on you.

Balaam may have had several problems, but one of the most serious was that he didn't recognize a teacher when he met one. And that, as I've already said, is our biggest problem in the School of Experience. Since the faculty ordinarily isn't listed in some catalog, we don't necessarily know who they are. Poor Balaam didn't know that his donkey was one of the teaching aides in the school. If he had recognized this, he would have taken note of what the donkey itself said: "Am I not your donkey, which you have ridden all your life to this day? Have I been in the habit of treating you this way?" (Numbers 22:30). Balaam would have said to himself, *This is a good and faithful donkey, so there must be some reason why it's acting just now in an unlikely way.*

Instead, Balaam got mad at the donkey. And that is so often our style. We curse the circumstances instead of learning from them. This is a main reason why we learn so little in the School of Experience. Not recognizing the faculty, we get angry with them instead of learning from them.

Of course there were reasons why Balaam did so. He had been seduced by success and by praise. The delegation that had come to him had told him how wonderful he was, so he wasn't in a good mood to learn. When we think too highly of ourselves, we're poor students. The process of learning always requires a certain measure of humility.

But on the other hand, we're also poor students when we think too little of ourselves. Self-despising doesn't help the learning process. We need a certain degree of self-respect, else we don't learn from experience; we're simply disheartened or defeated by it.

But the big secret is this: *Don't blame the donkey; fall in love with it.*

Here's what I mean. Most of us waste untold tons of emotional, mental, and spiritual energy hating our teachers and blaming them. I venture you have two friends who give completely contradicting reports on life and its faculty. They both come from seriously disadvantaged homes. Neither one had adequate clothing during their high school years. Both knew the embarrassment and the restrictions of poverty. One of these persons didn't know that he could learn from his experiences. He will tell you by the hour that he never really had a fair chance. He couldn't go to college. No one encouraged him to believe in himself. As far back as he can remember, the donkey has always been crushing his leg or falling beneath him. He hates the donkey. It has never occurred to him that the donkey might be a teacher, and a very good one.

Your other friend gives a different report. He tells you that when he saw how hard his father had to work and how little he had to show for his efforts, he resolved that he would find a better way of life. He remembers that people in his own neighborhood often made fun of him because of his dreams; they said he was uppity. And someone with advantages told him his dreams were grandiose; he was impressed by the very sound of the word, and he wondered where people picked up words of such eloquence. When he decided to pursue a college education, he discovered that he had all sorts of deficiencies; enough, in fact, to make him wonder if he should even try.

In truth, the donkey was giving him a rough ride. The donkey crushed him against any number of walls and sat down under him at a variety of crucial and embarrassing times. But he never blamed the donkey. At least, not for long. He simply kept asking himself what he could learn from his experiences.

It's pretty clear that your two friends were dealing with the same faculty. Both got some rough treatment. But one of them will go to his grave blaming the donkey, while the other will tell you how much he learned from the ride.

I won't tell you that everybody gets the same treatment in

the School of Experience. Some people, as far as I can see, get more than their share of the least-attractive faculty. When I review my own life, I think I've had some of the best and some of the worst; my faculty has been pretty well-distributed. But I see some people who seem to have gotten one tough teacher after another. Nevertheless, I've observed that it isn't a matter of who the faculty is. Not in the School of Experience! The whole issue, quite simply, is how we respond to our teachers. People who refuse to be responsible for themselves, who are looking for someone to blame, can always blame the faculty. They can tell you about every instance when the faculty has embarrassed them. They can bore you to tedium with their tales of misadventure and resentment. But others, with rather much the same faculty, will tell you that they wouldn't take a million dollars for their education.

I remember a Presbyterian minister who was blessed with a remarkable aunt. She was one of those transparently good human beings who never become famous except among the people who really get to know them. Whenever any passing misfortune came her way, she always said, "You know, this is going to do me a world of good." She had fallen in love with her donkey!

I don't know your circumstances. I have no idea who your faculty has been during the years of your study in the School of Experience. It's possible you've spent more time with sickness than I have or perhaps you have had more painful classes in bereavement. I wouldn't think of passing judgment on your faculty or on your response to their teaching because I haven't ridden your particular donkey—though it's possible I've ridden one very much like it.

But I have some counsel for you. As you mount your donkey, the donkey of your experiences, thank God for it and resolve that you will learn from it. This is a huge secret of happy, effective, victorious living: You don't run from your experiences; you embrace them. You don't kick your donkey; you ride it. Those who kick donkeys will get kicked in return. Those who ride donkeys generally reach their destination.

CHAPTER 5

When You've Been Given a Bad Name (Don't Let Others Define You)

1 SAMUEL 4:12-22: A man of Benjamin ran from the battle line, and came to Shiloh the same day, with his clothes torn and with earth upon his head. When he arrived, Eli was sitting upon his seat by the road watching, for his heart trembled for the ark of God. When the man came into the city and told the news, all the city cried out. When Eli heard the sound of the outcry, he said, "What is this uproar?" Then the man came quickly and told Eli. Now Eli was ninety-eight years old and his eyes were set, so that he could not see. The man said to Eli, "I have just come from the battle; I fled from the battle today." He said, "How did it go, my son?" The messenger replied, "Israel has fled before the Philistines, and there has also been a great slaughter among the troops; your two sons also, Hophni and Phinehas, are dead, and the ark of God has been captured." When he mentioned the ark of God, Eli fell over backward from his seat by the side of the gate; and his neck was broken and he died, for he was an old man, and heavy. He had judged Israel forty years.

Now his daughter-in-law, the wife of Phinehas, was pregnant, about to give birth. When she heard the news that the ark of God was captured, and that her father-in-law and her husband were dead, she bowed and gave birth; for her labor pains overwhelmed her. As she was about to die, the women attending her said to her, "Do not be afraid, for you have borne a son." But she did not answer or give heed. She named the child

Ichabod, meaning, "The glory has departed from Israel," because the ark of God had been captured and because of her father-in-law and her husband. She said, "The glory has departed from Israel, for the ark of God has been captured."

I've had a lifelong fascination with Ichabod. My mother, like most in her generation, had a limited formal education. But unlike many others, she loved to read, and now and then read fairly widely. Out of her knowledge of the nineteenth-century essayist and novelist Washington Irving, she found a name for me in those teenage years when I seemed to grow faster than Iowa corn in July. Looking at the way my arms extended, ungainly, beyond coat or jacket, she would say in despair, "You look just like Ichabod Crane!"

Ichabod Crane was the redoubtable hero of Irving's "The Legend of Sleepy Hollow," a village schoolteacher described as "tall, but exceedingly lank, with narrow shoulders, long arms and legs, hands that dangled a mile out of his sleeves, feet that might have served for shovels, and his whole frame most loosely hung together." On the whole, my mother had made a right connection: I was a younger edition of Ichabod Crane. And because I was an earnest Bible student I realized, even as a teenager, that Washington Irving had christened his hero for biblical reasons, though in the way he did so, he used a tragic story for comic purposes.

The nation of Israel was in one of its most depressed periods during the latter years of a judge named Eli. Most people who read their Bibles know Eli, if at all, for the fact that he was a mentor to young Samuel. Unfortunately, Eli wasn't as successful with his own sons as he was with Samuel. As his sons became comfortable in their priestly office, they exploited the office shamefully, even to the point of seducing women who came to worship. But instead of repenting, the two sons of Eli went still further. When Israel was losing a war with the Philistines, Hophni and Phinehas took to battle the sacred Ark of the Covenant, thinking they could use the most sacred object in their possession as a piece of magic, reasoning that it would ensure them victory in battle regardless of the nature of their relationship with God.

God can't be manipulated—a lesson we humans keep relearning. Not only was Israel defeated in the battle but also Hophni and Phinehas and great numbers of soldiers were killed and the Ark of the Covenant was captured by the Philistines. When the news of this multiple tragedy got back to Shiloh, Eli was so distraught that he fell over backward in anguish, breaking his neck and dying. At that time, Phinehas's wife, who is never named, was about to give birth. When the tragic news reached her—the news of her husband's and her father-in-law's deaths and the news of the loss of the ark of God—she "bowed and gave birth" (1 Samuel 4:19). When she appeared to be dying, a midwife tried to comfort her. "Do not be afraid, for you have borne a son" (1 Samuel 4:20). But the young woman was not to be comforted; the sense of tragedy was too great. She spoke only to name her new son, and she named him *Ichabod,* explaining, "The glory has departed from Israel, for the ark of God has been captured" (1 Samuel 4:22).

What do you do when your mother has named you Ichabod? It's nice fodder for a humorous writer like Washington Irving, and it may occasionally be fun as a conversation piece. But after a while one would weary of people asking, "Why did they name you 'The glory has departed'?" or "Is that *really* your name?"

We never hear about Ichabod again, except in a slanting reference. A generation later, one of the trusted leaders in Saul's army was a man named Ahijah, who is identified as a "son of Ahitub, Ichabod's brother, son of Phinehas son of Eli" (1 Samuel 14:3). This suggests that Ichabod had some kind of recognition factor among the people, otherwise the writer simply could have eliminated his name and continued, "son of Phinehas son of Eli." In truth, it's a circumlocution to introduce Ichabod's name. And we don't know why the writer did so. Maybe it was simply the human-interest factor; there's no story in Ahitub, but there is in Ichabod, even if it's a sorry one. Or maybe Ichabod later distinguished himself in some way, although one would think the writer would have said as much, since he bothered to mention his name.

No matter; it's a sorry name to carry all of your life, "The glory has departed." You ask yourself what kind of woman his mother was, that she would burden her son in such a way. I suspect you could say, at the least, that she was a better person than her husband, scoundrel that he was. She's surely more to be pitied than censured. Having borne her husband's infidelities and his abuse of his sacred office, then bearing a child at a time of personal and national tragedy, she had reason to be despondent. Probably some in our generation would think her naming was an act of superstition. It's possible, though I'm more inclined to think it was a devout act, an expression of her sacred despair that the cause of God had suffered embarrassment. There was probably some hopelessness mixed in with her feelings. I cast her with those Jewish women in Hitler's time who bore children while on their way to a concentration camp, or those women in several parts of the world in our time whose children have been born in refugee centers, while fleeing war or famine. If such a person names the child with accents of despair, I can only weep with them and pray for a better day.

I used to wonder if anyone other than a storyteller like Washington Irving would give the name *Ichabod* to a child. Almost surely some people have done so without knowing what they were doing. A good many less-than-desirable biblical names have been used by earnest people who wanted to give their child a biblical name and did so without due discrimination. Some years ago, while doing research on Wisconsin history, I discovered an instance of a mother who named her newborn son Ichabod with full attention to what she was doing. Her husband had died tragically only a short time before her son's birth. As a religious woman, she drew upon the Ichabod story of the Bible as symbolic of her own pain, at a time of both personal and national sorrow, and named her son Ichabod. He didn't let his name stand in his way. Ichabod Codding became a well-educated man, was ordained to the ministry, and gained honor in a limited way as a contributor to Wisconsin history. I admired him for rising above his name.

More recently, while vacationing in New England, I came upon another Ichabod, and again, a victorious one. Someone long ago named their son Ichabod Nichols, again with a sense that the glory had gone from life. Like Ichabod Codding, he came to feel a call to the ministry, and in time, he became the third pastor of First Parish in Portland, Maine. He served that congregation for nearly fifty years. A monument on the church grounds, in the heart of downtown Portland, pays him special honor. Not bad for an Ichabod.

I suspect we'll never know how many people have had to wrestle with the name they've been given. Some parents, with a sense of playfulness quite beyond my understanding, have chosen to play a child's given name off the peculiarities of the family name, and as a result the child's name always evokes some elements of ridicule. This kind of action is inane and inexcusable, and fortunately, it's rare.

The more frequent hazard of name-giving is more subtle. Literally millions of children, like Ichabod, are "named" by the circumstances of the world into which they're born. This is dramatically so for the child born into a world of famine or war. Such a child is sometimes so shaped by physical malnutrition as to never have a really healthy body. The child who loses a limb through the land mines on his or her playground will take a name through the rest of life, a name given not by the parents but by the culture that employs such evil instruments. And I hardly need mention that a great many children bear from birth a name given not by their parents' christening but by their parents' conduct. "Illegitimate child" is one of those names and surely one of the cruelest and most incorrect phrases in our speech.

There is no such thing as an illegitimate child, however illegitimate may be the conduct of the parents. I have often wondered how a child copes with the name it receives when the parent becomes a scandal, whether at the level of physical murder or public financial disgrace.

But such instances, tragic as they are, are dramatic and relatively infrequent. I'm thinking more particularly of children who get bad names from well-meaning parents. I knew a man whose abilities were average, but he never reached that high. Early on, older siblings began to call him Stupid, and his parents unwittingly augmented the problem. Instead of encouraging his modest gifts, they began to protect him from life's ordinary challenges. In time, he lived down to his name. Slow. Stupid.

Parents with high ambitions sometimes name their children more cruelly than they could ever dream. This can be especially true in those instances where parents try to live out their own unfulfilled dreams in the lives of their children. Arthur Miller gives a poignant example in his play "Death of a Salesman." Willy Loman has never won the success he so desperately sought, so now he places the burden on his sons, Happy and Biff, naming them to a throne he himself was not able to ascend. I wonder how many children have missed the *fun* of sports under the ambition of a father who wanted to live out in his offspring athletic honors he couldn't achieve? Or how many little girls have been entered in absurdly premature beauty and talent contests by unfulfilled mothers? So we name our children.

Sometimes we name them without our knowing it. A friend told me of a tremendously successful entrepreneur who in time brought his son into his business. But only part way. After some years the son, still struggling to find his place, analyzed his relationship with his father with the poignant sentence, "He never asked me any questions." By his silence the father was putting a name on his son. It might as well have been Ichabod.

I suspect I'm saying that Ichabod's story isn't as strange

and unlikely as at first it seems. True, not many of the people we know would think of burdening a child with a given name like *Failure* or *Bad News* or *Hard Times,* the way Ichabod's mother did. Not many have to worry about a name that evokes a raised eyebrow or a snicker, though the child whose last name identifies him or her with an infamous parent is as badly burdened. But I suspect no one could estimate how many of us bear our own version of *Ichabod.* Indeed, it is at this level that psychiatrists and counselors do some of their most intensive work as they sort through a patient's angers, resentments, fears, and humiliations. When a scientist suggested that some day parents might be sued by their children for allowing them to be born with their genetic defects, even those who are cynical about our litigious society probably raised an eyebrow. But I'm altogether certain that ten-thousands of people have maligned their parents, whether to a counselor or in late-night conversations with friends, as they've concluded that a parent made them an Ichabod—"The glory has departed."

As I said earlier, I don't know what the biblical Ichabod did with his name. I would like to think that perhaps he rose above it and that this is to be inferred from the later reference to his name in the book of 1 Samuel. I do know, as I've already said, that Wisconsin's Ichabod Codding brought honor to the name his mother gave him in an hour of deep sorrow, and so did Ichabod Nichols. And I have known literally hundreds of persons who have turned some sort of Ichabod into a badge of honor. One of the privileges of my many years as a pastor was the receiving of such stories. Sometimes the stories have come with tears or in such stillness that I've had to strain for every word. "My mother would beat me unmercifully while my father added to the humiliation by laughing. I vowed I would rise above it," a man said. But it had been a very long journey. In other instances, the narrator has so thoroughly won the battle that he laughs so hard, that I am soon laughing with him; tragedy has become comedy.

But I think nothing is better than a story Sawney Webb told so many times. After the Civil War, when the impoverished South desperately needed a new generation of leaders and when educational facilities were nearly nonexistent, Sawney Webb started a private prep school in Bell Buckle, Tennessee. But he couldn't make his school a place for "the rich and well-born," because at that time there weren't any rich in the area. Webb sought out boys who wanted to learn, and whenever he came upon one who was embarrassed by the lack of education and money in his family, the schoolmaster always said, "I want you to go out into the world and pedigree your ancestors."

In his story, Webb was referring to a horse he insisted he almost bought, a scrub horse. A poor farmer wanted to sell it for seventy-five dollars, explaining that he was "no blooded horse, but he sure has got the 'go' in him"; but Webb wanted a thoroughbred. The man who bought the scrub horse found he ran so furiously that he decided to give him a blooded horse's chance. He began to train and nurture him, and the little animal began to win races, so that in six months the man sold him for fourteen hundred dollars.

But that was only the beginning. In a few years, under still another owner, Major Brown, he was appearing on the Grand Circuit. On August 24, 1884, he set the world's pacing record for the mile. "Little Brown Jug," as the horse had become known, had become a legend. Major Brown sought out the horse's sire, Tom Hal, and found as many as possible of Hal's offspring, because horse lovers everywhere wanted to buy an animal from the same line as Little Brown Jug—the scrub horse that gave a pedigree to his ancestors (Laurence McMillin, *The Schoolmaker: Sawney Webb and the Bell Buckle Story* [Chapel Hill: The University of North Carolina Press, 1971], pp. 141-43).

The issue is not simply the names others give us (and our willingness to endorse such naming by accepting the judgments as if they were true) but, worse, the names we sometimes give to ourselves. And, sorry to say, some of us give worse names to ourselves than any thoughtless relative or enemy would ever do.

After contemplating hundreds of Ichabod stories, I have come to realize that no matter what name anyone has given us at birth or at some other sensitive time of life, we have to decide if we want to keep that name. In instances where I felt I dared, I've said, "Get over it! It's enough that this person has already hurt you for so many years. Don't let them keep you under a life sentence of death. It's time to take over your life."

Someone may have named you Ichabod. They may have done so thoughtlessly, or meanly, or even with good intentions. But you can change your name. By God's grace, you can claim in the courts of heaven a new and lovely name. That's part of what grace and redemption are all about.

CHAPTER 6

Color Her Moses
(Never Give Up. Never.)

MATTHEW 15:21-28: Jesus left that place and went away to the district of Tyre and Sidon. Just then a Canaanite woman from that region came out and started shouting, "Have mercy on me, Lord, Son of David; my daughter is tormented by a demon." But he did not answer her at all. And his disciples came and urged him, saying, "Send her away, for she keeps shouting after us." He answered, "I was sent only to the lost sheep of the house of Israel." But she came and knelt before him, saying, "Lord, help me." He answered, "It is not fair to take the children's food and throw it to the dogs." She said, "Yes, Lord, yet even the dogs eat the crumbs that fall from their masters' table." Then Jesus answered her, "Woman, great is your faith! Let it be done for you as you wish." And her daughter was healed instantly.

*I*f I were an artist, I think I would want most of all to paint the interesting faces in the passing crowds. I would park my car on a street where pedestrians were finding their way. The location could be either a small town or a city, as long as a fair number is walking by. A shopping mall isn't quite as good because shopping, by its focusing, distracts people from their wholeness. If I were an artist, I would try to catch the light in their eyes and the laughter on their lips. I would look for the lines of strain in the texture of the neck and the little touches of petulance about the corners of the mouth, the wrinkles of contentment around the eyes, and the signs of deep weariness just back of the eye. I would look for persons with stories in their faces. Stories are always there, you know. Sometimes we do a good job of keeping them hidden, but a really able artist can find them. If I were an artist, I would look for such stories. Then I could write a whole novel in a painting of just one face.

If I had been an artist in Jesus' day, there's one person in particular I would have wanted to sketch. Her name isn't mentioned in the Bible, but tradition says she was called Justa, and that her daughter's name was Bernice. We don't know her age or anything about her physical appearance. By nationality, she was a Canaanite, a Syrian woman from Phoenicia, as the Gospel of Mark reports it.

In painting her, we must depend almost entirely on our own imagination. Height, age, complexion, hair, eyes, form, carriage—all of these are left to our probing mind. Only one thing is sure: coloring. *Color her Moses.* And if you say, "*Moses?* There's no such color as Moses," I will dare to reply, "There is now." After all, in the spectrum of colors, we have a shade called *titian*; it's a color that got its name from the sixteenth-century Venetian painter Tiziano Vecellio—more familiarly known as Titian—who used a particular color with such skill that we've given it his name. So it is that I would use Moses' name for the color I have in mind, because Moses brought a distinctive moral coloring to a certain incident.

My color isn't really in the spectrum of physical light and dark nor in the realm of visible phenomena. I'm thinking of the color of a temperament, the hue of character; call it a spiritual color, if you will. I think you know what I mean. We sometimes say, "I feel a little *blue* today." Thus we describe an intellectual or emotional mood by the medium of a visible color. That's what I mean when I say I would color this woman *Moses.* I see in her the same quality of unrelenting character that showed itself long ago in the man who led the nation of Israel out of Egypt's bondage.

Let me tell you this woman's story, then perhaps, with my also telling you of an incident from the life of Moses, you will see why I want to color this woman Moses. As I said a moment ago, this woman was a Canaanite. To us, that means little. In Jesus' day it meant a great deal to any Jew. The Canaanites were not simply Gentiles, they were considered the worst of the Gentiles because they were ancestral enemies of the Jewish people and, as such, people held in reproach.

The woman met Jesus on what was apparently the only occasion when he was outside of Palestine. He had withdrawn from the mounting crowds that were constantly following him back in his own country, and he had come to the district of Tyre and Sidon. Jesus' life and ministry were drawing near the end. The crowds were cheering him with ever more excitement, but at the same time the opposition of Jesus' enemies was increasing. It seems clear that Jesus knew how near they were to a crucial showdown, and it's likely that he had chosen this time to slip away with his disciples for a brief period that might restore his soul in preparation for the crisis ahead.

Instead, Jesus found himself with an immediate crisis right there in his path. The crisis is a woman, probably physically small, yet somehow formidable. She's shouting. "Have mercy on me, Lord, Son of David; my daughter is tormented by a demon" (Matthew 15:22). It's a pathetic cry. Anytime a child is seriously ill, a parent feels a certain innate helplessness, and when the sickness is a dramatically deranged personality, the sense of helplessness is even greater. The people of Jesus' day called it *demon possession.* This was their graphic way of saying that the person's conduct seemed to come from hell itself, that their actions couldn't be explained by normal earthly patterns. When the daughter was in such a state, it must have been difficult for the mother even to realize that this was, in fact, her child.

Savage and violent, depressed and self-destructive, she sometimes seemed hardly human, let alone a member of the family. There were no psychiatrists in those days, no treatments, no "wonder drugs." But the mother had heard somewhere that Jesus was capable of dealing with even such extreme cases, so she came to him in pathetic, desperate hope.

I feel empathy for this woman. I feel it as a father and a grandfather; I know how desperate a parent can feel. I also remember, from my days as a pastor, how I sometimes dreaded visits to the pediatric ward of the hospital. The pathos of a suffering child is almost more than one can bear. I feel particular empathy for this woman because I'm struck by something that isn't mentioned. Where is the father? Should we conclude that she is a single mother? If so, is it because the father has died? Or could it be that he has abandoned her and the girl, perhaps because he feels the stigma of the child's illness, especially in a culture where the illness may be seen as a result of the sins of the parents. Or is the father willing enough to be here with his wife and child but financially unable to make the trip; someone has to feed the family, you know. In any event, when I hear the woman in our story cry to Jesus, "Have mercy! My daughter is severely possessed by a demon," I expect the Master to show the compassion that he seemed to give so extravagantly to every kind of human need.

Instead, Jesus ignores the woman. The Gospel writer says, "But he did not answer her at all" (Matthew 15:23). Here is a distraught, brokenhearted mother, making a last-ditch appeal for her child, and Jesus doesn't even acknowledge her. This bothers the disciples, but not the way I wish it had. The woman makes them nervous. They plead with Jesus to send her away because "she keeps shouting after us." I'm sorry they didn't feel compassion for her, only irritation at the inconvenience she was causing.

But instead of sending the woman away as the disciples had requested, Jesus told the disciples why he wasn't healing her. This is itself an interesting response because the disciples weren't asking for an explanation; they were only saying, "Let's get rid of her." But Jesus explained, "I was sent only to the lost sheep of the house of Israel" (Matthew 15:24).

If the woman heard this theological explanation, she wasn't deterred by it. Instead, she came and knelt in front of Jesus and said simply, *"Lord, help me."* I can't imagine a more persuasive appeal. But Jesus turned to her and said, "It is not fair to take the children's food and throw it to the dogs" (Matthew 15:26). To our ears, Jesus' answer seems insensitive, but the woman knew what Jesus was saying. The Jews of Jesus' day often spoke of all other ethnic groups as "dogs"— "Gentile dogs," "infidel dogs." It was not a kind term. In that world, dogs were street scavengers: hungry, savage, diseased curs that ate the refuse of the gutters. But as New Testament Greek reports the conversation, there was an unlikely suggestion of encouragement in Jesus' statement. He didn't use the customary word for dog, but the diminutive, the word that described a household pet or puppy.

The mother settled on that tiny detail as if it were the hope of her life. "Yes, Lord, yet even the dogs eat the crumbs that fall from their masters' table" (Matthew 15:27).

How can you resist this woman? Color her Moses! How can you say no to someone who turns your denial into a reason for acceptance? She has appealed to her child's one hope, and he has ignored her. She has knelt at his feet and begged, and he has replied that what he has to give he must save for the children, not for the likes of her. And with marvelous wit she says, in effect, "True, I'm a Gentile dog. But I'm staying close to the table, where even a dog—a puppy like me!—can have the crumbs that fall. And crumbs are all I need. Crumbs will do for me." And isn't it interesting that this woman said, "the crumbs that fall from *their masters'* table"? She was laying a claim on Jesus, a declaration of relationship. A dog she might be, but she was *his* dog! She had a claim on this table, pathetic though it appeared.

Jesus answered, "Woman, great is your faith! Let it be done for you as you wish." And her daughter was healed at that very moment (Matthew 15:28).

The point of this story, it seems to me, is this: What do you believe when heaven is silent? When God's response, whether by silence or by the kind of negation this woman received, seems a contradiction to what God is, then what do you do? The experience is not an unusual one. Almost all of us have known some devastating time in life when we've prayed for what seemed reasonable and best but found heaven to be silent or the circumstances themselves to speak in God's stead as a sullen *no*.

Even the greatest saints have struggled with this experience. C. S. Lewis, the British scholar whose books have now for two to three generations helped literally millions of people, watched his cherished wife, Joy, die of cancer. He wrote,

> Go to Him when your need is desperate, when all other help is vain, and what do you find? A door slammed in your face, and a sound of bolting and double bolting on the inside. After that, silence. You may as well turn away. The longer you wait, the more emphatic the silence will become. There are no lights in the windows. It might be an empty house. Was it ever inhabited? It seemed so once. And that seeming was as strong as this. (C. S. Lewis, *A Grief Observed* [New York: Seabury Press, 1961], p. 9)

In time, Lewis found the solace of God, so much so that he said it would be "wicked" to call his wife back from the world she had now entered. But first there was this silence, this door bolted and double bolted. What do you do at such a time? What do you do when it looks as if heaven is contrary to its own character?

The great Moses came to such an hour. His people, the fledgling nation of Israel, had forsaken God, and God said to Moses, "Now let me alone, so that my wrath may burn hot against them and I may consume them" (Exodus 32:10). But Moses argued with God, reminded God of the promises made at another time, challenged God about the divine character.

So what do you do when God is silent or when God rebuffs? You knock more loudly! What do you do when life seems to say, "You're a dog, and God doesn't care about you"? You ask God again. You chide God with your own form of gallows humor. What do you do when God himself seems to be out of character? You believe in what God is, in utter, faith-driven contradiction of the circumstances.

Back to our first-century street scene, where a wisp of a mother, all alone, dares on her daughter's behalf to challenge Jesus of Nazareth. She addresses Jesus as Lord, asking his help, and he ignores her. She asks again, and he brushes her off with a statement about dogs. Then she replies, "But even the dogs can have the crumbs from their masters' table," and I think I hear her saying, "I know what God is like, and I know what you are like. You're not like these circumstances make you seem to be. You're not like the rejection I'm supposed to feel. I believe in you even if it seems you don't want me to." When you hear such a prayer, color this woman *Moses*; she is praying a Moses-like prayer. She insists on believing in who God is, in spite of what God seems at that moment to be.

The Bible says that Jesus marveled at the faith of this Canaanite woman. She had looked circumstances full in the face, circumstances that said *no*. Still worse, the circumstances said that God didn't care. But she replied, in effect, God *must* care, because that is God's nature. Color her *Moses,* because she cares enough about her daughter and believes enough in God that she won't stop praying.

I don't have to tell you how much you and I need this kind of faith. We need it at a worldwide level as we deal with issues of war, poverty, and monstrous epidemics. But we need it also at very private and intimate levels in the issues of family and friends and the issues of our own lives, issues which, at times, are so intimate that we are afraid to speak them aloud. If at such times we seem to be greeted by a vast silence or by a sense of rejection, we must take hold. Like the Canaanite woman, we cry out to God still more insistently.

Watch this Canaanite woman now, as she walks away. Watch even the contours of her back, because they will add something to our painting of her face. Now she begins to run, for joy. Her daughter is well! Even yet I can't tell whether this woman is short or tall, slight or sturdy. I only know that she believes in God and that she loves her daughter too much to give up in the face of presumed rejection. Color her Moses.

CHAPTER 7

Plot for a Life
(More Than Success)

MARK 10:46-52: They came to Jericho. As he and his disciples and a large crowd were leaving Jericho, Bartimaeus son of Timaeus, a blind beggar, was sitting by the roadside. When he heard that it was Jesus of Nazareth, he began to shout out and say, "Jesus, Son of David, have mercy on me!" Many sternly ordered him to be quiet, but he cried out even more loudly, "Son of David, have mercy on me!" Jesus stood still and said, "Call him here." And they called the blind man, saying to him, "Take heart; get up, he is calling you." So throwing off his cloak, he sprang up and came to Jesus. Then Jesus said to him, "What do you want me to do for you?" The blind man said to him, "My teacher, let me see again." Jesus said to him, "Go; your faith has made you well." Immediately he regained his sight and followed him on the way.

*O*ut in the harbor of New York City stands the fabled Lady Liberty. Through all kinds of changing fortunes, she remains a worldwide symbol of hope, of freedom, of possible new beginnings. But at another place in the harbor there is an island with a very different message. Every weekday, a ferryboat plows its steady, sullen way there with its sorry cargo.

This is Hart Island, with its Potter's Field. There have been over three quarters of a million burials on Hart Island since Potter's Field was established there in 1869. Currently, up to three thousand persons a year are buried there (William E. Geist, "The Unwanted," in *The Last Word: The New York Times Book of Obituaries and Farewells; A Celebration of Unusual Lives*, ed. Marvin Siegel [New York: William Morrow, 1997], p. 424). The coffins are stacked three deep in trenches that are eight feet deep, fifty feet long, and twenty feet wide. These are the unwanted, some of them infants, some adults. About once a week someone comes out to claim a body that has already been buried—claimed by someone who has discovered late that their family member has died without their knowing it and has been buried in near anonymity (Michael Ellison, "Only the Lonely," *The Guardian Weekend*, Saturday, June 5, 1999).

Hart Island and its Potter's Field bother me. Actually, they bother me twice over. I'm something of an idealist about America, so I hate to confess that people can die in our country, daily, with the American dream not even remotely fulfilled. But as a Christian, I'm bothered even more. I insist on believing that there is a grand story in every person's life, just waiting to happen. An undeveloped novelist in me wants to work out the plotline for every life I see: a human being of life and potential, perhaps wrestling with profound adversity—yes, even, perhaps with a plot that concludes with apparent tragedy—and yet, with a certain dignity and purpose. Whether I laugh or cry at the end of the story, I have to know that the person mattered. I have to see a plot.

Peggy Noonan, who was special assistant to President Ronald Reagan and whose observations often appear in op-ed pages in publications like *The Wall Street Journal*, tells of the time when she prayed for a miracle. She confesses that she believes in miracles. "The way I see it," she writes, "life isn't flat and thin and 'realistic,' it's rich and full of mystery and surprise" (Peggy Noonan, *What I Saw at the Revolution: A Political Life in the Reagan Era* [New York: Random House, 1990], p. 32). I feel the same way. I don't think life is flat, I think it's bursting with meaning and purpose. I think there's a plot waiting to unfold.

It's that conviction that draws me to the story in the tenth chapter of Mark's Gospel. I readily recognize that, at the outset of the story, we're looking, in Bartimaeus, at a life that is flat and that will probably end in the first-century equivalent of Hart Island. If I am to find a plotline for this human being (indeed, if there is any *hope* of a plotline), it will be flat as a prairie in western Kansas, with no turning or unfolding. Just a line that will fade out somewhere on an uncertain horizon, a potential plot that never really comes to pass.

The Gospel writer tells us that the man's name is Bartimaeus, son of Timaeus. That, of itself, suggests a plot going nowhere. You see, "Bar-Timaeus" means "Son of Timaeus." So when we're told that the man's name is Bartimaeus, son of Timaeus, we get the feeling he's a bit of a blur on the screen of life. We reason that he must have once had another name, like John, Peter, or Andrew, so that his name was really John bar Timaeus or Peter bar Timaeus. To say that he was Bartimaeus, son of Timaeus, works only if his name were like some of those wonderful Welsh names, like William Williams or Robert Roberts. Not so for this man. I suspect that whatever first name he once had was forgotten somewhere along the way. Now he's known simply as the son of Timaeus.

And when the introductory sentence is complete, we know at least one reason why this man's name is obscure. We are told that he is a blind beggar who sits by the roadside plying his trade. I sense that people choose to forget his name, as if by forgetting it they have disposed of him. I knew a man once who did that with the people he didn't like. He remembered names with admirable skill, but not those he didn't want to; they were always "that fellow out in Texas," or "that woman in western Kentucky." You diminish someone's plot in a hurry when you can make them anonymous.

And Bartimaeus was that kind of person. He was a blind man in a culture that had no provision for the blind or the physically or mentally challenged. People believed that such persons couldn't contribute to life, and, therefore, someone would have to care for them, unless they'd beg. So they begged. Worse yet, some of the most discerning people—the kind who established standards of common judgment—saw a philosophical significance in the problems a person like Bartimaeus suffered. These scholars reasoned that if an individual had suffered some tragedy or serious limitation, whether at birth or in later developments, it was evidence that God was displeased with that person. And if that's the case, hard logic says, it's better to get them out of mind, if possible. Their presence complicates our understanding of life, so let's be done with them. We'll begin by forgetting their name, or part of it, and in time we can probably forget all of it. Then we can refer to the person simply as "that blind beggar." Eventually, even that distinction can go, and we'll say, "That fellow by the side of the road."

There. Now there's no chance of a plot for this life.

And that's the way this story, the story of a man named Bartimaeus, was going to unfold. But let me tell you a little more about him. We discover, as the story unfolds, that Bartimaeus wasn't born blind, because when Jesus asks him what he wants, the man answers, "I want to see *again.*" And when he's healed, we're told that he *"regained* his sight" (emphasis added, see Mark 10:51-52). So he wasn't born blind, although we have no hint as to how he lost his sight, nor how long he had been blind.

We have further insight into Bartimaeus's sorrow by our knowledge that he became blind at some point in his life rather than being born blind. If he had been born blind, he wouldn't have had a measurable loss to regret, a comparison of loss to reflect upon. But Bartimaeus had once enjoyed sight and somehow had lost it. Probably it was through disease. Diseases of the eye were commonplace in the first-century world. Whatever the story, now he was doomed to this state—not simply of blindness, difficult as that would be, but also of begging and of the reproach of people who saw him as under the disfavor of God. So you can see that there's no plot in this man's life. His story is not going anywhere. He is the kind of person who will someday be buried in the first-century equivalent of Hart Island, virtually unknown and easily forgotten—unmissed and unmourned. This is especially true when so many might prefer to forget the person—this person, Bartimaeus, with no plot to his life, a life not going anywhere.

But you never know when a life without purpose or significance may get a plot. It happened to the son of Timaeus. He heard that Jesus of Nazareth was traveling the road nearby, perhaps a road where he often begged. So he stationed himself along the road, and when he heard that Jesus was near, he began to cry out for this Son of David to have mercy on him. It wasn't an eloquent prayer, not in the shape of its words, that is. No matter; it proved very powerful. Madeleine L'Engle, the novelist and essayist, recalls that when she hovered for days between life and death after an automobile accident, she could utter only the Jesus prayer—"Lord Jesus Christ, have mercy on me" (*The Rock that Is Higher: Story as Truth* [Wheaton, Ill.: Harold Shaw, 1993], p. 13). I was fascinated that this woman who deals in words had no eloquence while at death's entryway. She used one of the oldest, and surely one of the simplest, prayers in the ritual of our human race. And so it was with Bartimaeus.

And Jesus stopped, talked with him, and healed him. And Bartimaeus, in turn, rose up to follow Jesus. So it was that a blind man regained his sight, and a beggar regained his dignity. Most of all, so it was that Bartimaeus got a story. He got a plot for his life.

I know that someone is registering an objection just now. You're wondering if I'm saying that a blind beggar doesn't have a plot, while with his sight, the plot is restored. No, that's not at all what I mean. In truth, if Bartimaeus had called out to Jesus, and Jesus had spoken to him but had chosen not to heal him, I submit that nevertheless his life would have gotten a plot. Quite simply, quite baldly and boldly, I'm saying that Jesus Christ gives a plot to life. Jesus once said a very daring, almost outrageous thing about him-

self: "I am the way, and the truth, and the life" (John 14:6).
That is, he was saying, "*I am the plot*. Without me, life is flat
and thin, and dreadfully 'realistic,' but I give it purpose,
meaning, and eternal value."

I am trying to say that when we call Jesus the Savior, we're
calling him the Plot Giver. And I say this precisely because I
believe that life is more than a flatness. I believe that you
and I are eternal, and that Jesus touches this eternal chord
in our lives, and that he does so as no one else can.

I say this with a prejudice. I speak out of my experience,
and that prejudices my outlook. Almost every summer I make
a pilgrimage to my hometown, Sioux City, Iowa. There I will
do what I have done so many times before. I will park the car
on Helmer Street. Then I'll pause to look at the house where
my boyhood friend, Ed, lived so very long ago. I'll walk slowly,
deliberately up the hill to stand by Ralph's house, then half a
block farther to Phil's. Then I'll make my way back to the
heart of it all, 2019 West Palmer Street, and I will stand for as
long as I dare, simply staring at that poor box of a house. I
will remember that winter that bridged my tenth and
eleventh years, a winter in the worst of the Great Depression.

One Sunday night late that fall I had listened to an evangelist preach at a neighborhood church and had somewhat
fearfully made my way to the altar, where I asked God to for-
give my sins and to save me. That night my life got a *plot*, an
eternal plot. From that time on, it was going somewhere.

So each summer when I make my hometown pilgrimage, I
wonder about Ed, Ralph, and Phil. They were great kids! I
wonder if they're still living, but even more, I wonder if their
lives got a plot. Understand me: I'm not wondering if they
succeeded; I find our definitions of success too fuzzy to matter. But I wonder if they got a plot in their lives? Did their
lives move from flat and thin to uplifted, lofty, and eternal?

The late Mother Teresa would know what I'm trying to
say. As you know, she and her associates so often picked up
near-corpses from the street and brought them into a clean,
warm, comfortable place to die. At first people ridiculed

what Mother Teresa was doing. After all, most of the people she rescued died anyway before the night was over, or within a few days, so what had she accomplished?

Mother Teresa said simply that she had given them a place to die in God's love, a place where they mattered. I want to say that she gave their lives, even at the end, *a plot*. The persons she and her team rescued were no longer meaningless flotsam and jetsam; they were eternal creatures with a purpose and a magnificent destiny.

But I sense that I'm still leaving a possible confusion. Because I mentioned earlier about the anonymous dead who are buried on Hart Island and now about those whom Mother Teresa and her aides picked up from the city streets, I may have given a wrong impression. You could easily conclude that my concern is focused on the desperately poor, the souls who live out on the margins of economic and social life, so let me say more surely what I have in mind.

Because I travel a great deal, I spend many hours in the executive waiting rooms of airports. I travel enough to gain this privilege free of charge. In those executive rooms, the people around me are very important. They sometimes tell me so. They have cell phones, computers, attaché cases, and the appurtenances of busyness.

But as I watch them chattering on their cell phones, sending out their email, and hurrying to the next flight, I ask myself if there's a plot in their lives. Are their lives any less flat than those who are wheeled out to Hart Island, or those picked up from the streets by the Mother Teresas?

No. Not unless eternity breaks in. Not unless they meet the Savior, the One who gives our lives a plot. An *eternal* plot. And that, in a word, is who Jesus is. He is the One who comes into our human lives, if we will let him, so that our lives will be delivered from the flat and the thin and will be set free to be eternal—on Hart Island, or in the executive suite, or anywhere in between. Jesus gives life a plot, a going-somewhere, a going to God.

Amen.

CHAPTER 8

Party Gone Flat
(What to Do When Life Loses Its Flavor)

JOHN 2:1-11: On the third day there was a wedding in Cana of Galilee, and the mother of Jesus was there. Jesus and his disciples had also been invited to the wedding. When the wine gave out, the mother of Jesus said to him, "They have no wine." And Jesus said to her, "Woman, what concern is that to you and to me? My hour has not yet come." His mother said to the servants, "Do whatever he tells you." Now standing there were six stone water jars for the Jewish rites of purification, each holding twenty or thirty gallons. Jesus said to them, "Fill the jars with water." And they filled them up to the brim. He said to them, "Now draw some out, and take it to the chief steward." So they took it. When the steward tasted the water that had become wine, and did not know where it came from (though the servants who had drawn the water knew), the steward called the bridegroom and said to him, "Everyone serves the good wine first, and then the inferior wine after the guests have become drunk. But you have kept the good wine until now." Jesus did this, the first of his signs, in Cana of Galilee, and revealed his glory; and his disciples believed in him.

I knew that "Life is real! life is earnest!" long before I read Henry Wadsworth Longfellow. You couldn't grow up in the Iowa of my boyhood without being impressed by life's reality and earnestness. Iowa taught one that the winters were cold, the summers were hot, but the soil was fertile, and if you worked hard, you'd get a crop. You learned this in Iowa even if you grew up in a city, as I did, because the mood of the farm dominated everything in the state.

Nevertheless, with all that earnestness, still we laughed a lot at my house. My dad had a good sense of humor, and although Mother didn't always get his remarks, she had learned to laugh as if she did. And we went to church, where we laughed a good deal. Not so much on Sunday mornings; Sunday mornings tended to be circumspect and orderly, even if we didn't have a printed order of worship. But the testimony services often had a tone that varied from confessionally humorous to jubilant, and the frequent revival services were abundant in robust singing, simple jokes, and general goodwill. I was blessed from my early days with the impression that church was a place of glad restoration. We might come tired and disheartened, but we generally went home smiling and hopeful.

But I think I've had a problem all my life in holding together these two elements, my Iowa earnestness and my Christian gladness. In truth, they go together very well, but I've sometimes had a hard time realizing as much. The story in John's Gospel, about Jesus' miracle at the wedding feast, symbolizes my problem.

To begin with, I had no basis for understanding a Middle Eastern wedding. The weddings I had seen would have made Lake Wobegon look bacchanalian. Our weddings were as pretty and pleasant as we could make them, but they were wisely frugal; folks reasoned that money spent on decorations and refreshments could be better applied toward the first month's rent or as a down payment on a used car. We couldn't have imagined weddings that extended over several days, as did even ordinary weddings in Jesus' day.

Specifically, the wedding of a virgin was required by first-century Jewish law to take place on a Wednesday. The events then continued for seven days. The ceremony itself took place on the evening of the first day following a feast, after which the couple were led to their new home. There they stayed for a week, while guests stopped by each day, some probably coming more than once. In the Middle East, hospitality is an absolute must. If you've traveled in the area, you know that the moment you stop in a tiny shop to look even casually at an item, the owner insists on your having tea. In the case of a wedding, wine was the order of the day. William Barclay said that the point was never heavy drinking; in fact, he noted that the wine was served in a mixture composed of two parts of wine to three parts of water (William Barclay, *The Gospel of John, Vol. 1*, The Daily Study Bible Series [Philadelphia: Westminster Press, 1956], p. 82). Hospitality was the issue.

Thus, to run out of supplies—especially wine—was the kind of breach of conduct that would be a matter of village gossip for the next generation. And that was the predicament as this story began to unfold. Jesus and several of his disciples had come to a wedding at Cana of Galilee, just a short distance from Nazareth. Apparently Jesus' mother had some significant tie to the family, because when the family ran out of wine, it was Mary who asked Jesus to solve the problem and who then ordered the servants to do whatever Jesus asked them to do. One tradition, out of ancient Coptic records, says that Mary was a sister to the bridegroom's mother. Whatever the case, she obviously felt enough responsibility to exert some authority.

Nor was she cautious in the use of her authority. When Jesus demurred, saying that his time had not yet come (a way, in John's Gospel, of saying that it was not yet the time for a display of his power or glory), Mary waved aside his objection and told the servants to do whatever Jesus asked them to do.

You know the story of the miracle that followed. Jesus told the servants to fill six of the huge stone water jars with water. The Gospel reports that they proceeded to fill them "to the brim"; that is, there was no room for another substance to be added. When the water was served to the steward of the occasion, he marveled. "Everyone serves the good wine first, and then the inferior wine after the guests have become drunk. But you have kept the good wine until now" (John 2:10).

It was a remarkable moment. John's Gospel says this was "the first of [Jesus'] signs," and that it "revealed his glory; and his disciples believed in him" (John 2:11). The inference is that thus far Jesus' disciples had admired him as a teacher to whom they were attaching themselves, but this experience put him in a whole new light. The writer doesn't explain what he means by the phrase "believed in him," but it's clear that their perception of Jesus had moved up to an entirely new level.

But with my inbred sense of earnestness and purpose, I always wondered why "the first" of Jesus' signs should come at something like a wedding celebration. Raising Lazarus from the dead, healing a leper or a blind man, or having a crucial showdown with the Pharisees strikes me as an appropriate first sign. But *providing wine at a wedding?* What does *this* have to do with establishing the kingdom of heaven? How is this event the beginning of a new age? If this is a sign, and the first at that, what is it a sign *of?*

In a sublime, mystical sense, this miracle at the Cana wedding may point us to the grand consummation of all things. In his parables, Jesus pictured the kingdom of heaven through the picture of a wedding banquet. In one instance he told of a king who gave a wedding banquet for his son, a signal event but one that for some strange reason, those invited refused to attend. At last the king had to gather in "all whom they found, both good and bad; so the wedding hall was filled with guests" (Matthew 22:10). In another parable, Jesus focused attention on the bridesmaids who were in the wedding party, five of whom in their wisdom were prepared for the long wait and five who in their foolishness were without lamp oil enough to last through the night (see Matthew 25:1-13). In both parables, the potentially happy occasion of a wedding was clouded by some shortfall, so to speak—in one, by the irrational failure of invited guests to respond to the invitation, and in the other, by the thoughtlessness of some bridesmaids to be properly ready for the occasion. The apostle Paul also used a wedding as his figure of speech when he spoke of the church (the body of believers) as the wife of Christ (see Ephesians 5:21-30).

The concept comes to its full expression in the closing chapters of the book of Revelation. When the age-long battle between good and evil moves to its end, the victory is celebrated at "the marriage supper of the Lamb," where the people of God constitute the bride, "clothed / with fine linen, bright and pure" (see Revelation 19:7-9). I think it's reasonable to see a tie between the miracle at the Cana wedding and the continuing theme of a wedding as a symbol of God's victorious purposes in our world. It isn't the kind of tie one should use to make a legal case but the kind that an artist would establish in symbols throughout a painting or a composer would employ in the recurring motif or "submotif" of a symphony. Considering the nature of John's Gospel, it's especially easy to see such a possible connection. John makes clear from the outset that his book will not be fenced in by the usual boundaries of time, space, and literalism. For John, the event at the marriage in Cana is not simply a miracle, but a *sign,* pointing to something of greater significance beyond itself.

But I've never been happy with a perception of Christianity that is, as someone has said, "so heavenly minded as to be of no earthly use." So while I suspect there was a breathtaking purpose in what happened that day at a simple wedding feast, I want to know if there is more than that. Sometimes when we look at some simple matter we know we should look further, to see the deeper meaning. This time I'm suggesting that we move back from the deeper meaning to find the simpler one.

I'm satisfied that there is such a lesson. I'm impressed that this first *sign* happened at a perfectly human celebration, a somewhat frivolous event where people had probably spent beyond their means, where the humor was unsophisticated and the laughter more raucous than delicate. The sign didn't occur at a meeting of philosophers, or of political or economic movers and shakers; it happened at a village party. I like that! It's hard on my Iowa earnestness, but it feels like the revival laughter of my boyhood.

The fact is, the party was in danger of going flat. Perhaps the parents, poor peasant folk, had planned skimpily. Some of us remember meals when our mothers warned us not to take a second helping because if we did, there wouldn't be enough for our guests. Maybe that's what had happened. Or perhaps some of the village folk had brought out-of-town family with them. One way or another, a modest family was about to be humiliated. So is that a big deal? Who cares?

John's Gospel says Jesus cared. Prodded by his mother, Jesus invested his unique energy to save a family from embarrassment and to restore life to a party.

That's a quite significant word for the kind of world in which many of us live. I keep reading about the boredom that inflicts a current generation of Americans and Europeans. Surfeited by creature comforts and spectacle, dazzled by variety and choice, they're *bored*. Their party has gone flat. Erich Fromm, the landmark twentieth-century psychiatrist, said, "Man is the only animal that can be bored" (*The Sane Society* [New York: Holt, Rinehart and Winston, 1955], p. 24). I venture that this is because only we humans have a sense of something beyond ourselves. The more we have of life's tangibles, the more we grasp for some intangibles that satisfy us in an ultimate way.

I believe that when Jesus Christ comes into our lives, he not only saves us for an eternity after death, he brings eternity into our lives here and now. To the degree that we allow our Lord to do so, he helps us to sleep better, eat better, talk better, love better, and laugh better. He brings a kind of continual excitement into life. The Christian life is wonderfully earthly; we don't seek, in our beliefs, to escape from this life, but we do expect to get hold of something beyond this earth. Not simply when we die; heavens, no! We expect a quite out-of-this-world touch on our lives here.

Sometimes when I look out on a congregation where I have come to be the guest preacher, I am distressed by many of the faces I see. I'm not speaking of those persons who carry heavy loads; in truth, I've learned that the burdened people don't necessarily look burdened and distressed. I'm thinking of those persons who look as if church is a root canal experience without anesthesia. For such persons I wish Jesus would suddenly appear and let them know that this faith they profess to follow is full of life, *abundant* life! I'm with Teresa of Avila, who prayed to be delivered from "frowning saints." In truth, of course, "frowning saints" is an oxymoron. Saints have found the springs of laughter.

And I'm impressed that Jesus' miracle took place not just at a wedding but at a wedding in a small Middle Eastern village, at a gathering of what society would call simple folk. I'm glad miracles don't necessarily happen in headline places with headline people who have publicity agents.

I once had such a miracle. I was seventeen years old, only a few months out of high school and now a student in a little Bible school. These were the latter days of the Great Depression. I had come to school with enough money to cover tuition, board, and room for seven or eight weeks. After that, it would be a matter of faith, though I knew the school wouldn't put me out. I had one pair of shoes. They had worn through to the point that I was stuffing cardboard in the soles to protect my feet from the ground.

I had another pair of shoes, but they didn't fit. My pastor, the Reverend Reginald D. Acheson, had given them to me. They were good shoes, better than I could buy, but slightly used. For some reason, they didn't satisfy my pastor. Unfortunately, they didn't fit me. I tried and tried to squeeze my feet in, but it couldn't be done. So late one autumn Saturday, my roommate and I went to a little shoe shop on a side street in a somewhat dismal neighborhood, a place that both bought and sold shoes, new and used. I said I wanted to buy a pair of shoes. The shopkeeper showed me a pair, inexpensive but brand new, and they fit. Now I opened my paper bag and asked how much he could allow me in trade for these good but slightly used shoes. He examined them and said he'd give me the new pair for my pair and a dollar.

This may sound to you like a very good deal, but for me it was the end. All I had in the world, I had in my pocket: one very small dime. Going shopping under such circumstances was absurd, but when you're young, desperate, and possessed of some touch of faith, you sometimes try absurd things. I thanked the shopkeeper, put Mr. Acheson's shoes back in the bag, and headed out the door. But suddenly the shopkeeper said, "I'll trade you even-up, son."

I now have several pairs of shoes, but nothing like the pair I took out of the shop that Saturday afternoon. That's a silly little story, isn't it? It will never find a place in a book of miracles or one of those angel accounts. But each time I think of it, I see Jesus transforming a party gone flat into a place of rare celebration. I'm profoundly grateful that the God of the universe cares about simple folk, with simple needs, in village events that don't merit a visit from the society reporter.

I'm very sure that when the writer of John's Gospel tells us the story of the wedding miracle at Cana of Galilee, he has something very big in mind. After all, he calls the miracle the first of Jesus' signs. But in and through the story, I see the wonder of God's concern for human beings for whom life's party has gone flat. And when I see such persons, whether on skid row or the Harvard campus, I want to tell them that Jesus the Christ can bring a whole new dimension to life—life eternal and abundant. To a world of ennui and boredom, to a world where there's no party, Jesus brings the wonder of celebration and excitement. I want to tell them that the Christian life is indeed real and earnest, but it is also deep, wide, and high. Especially, it's *high*.

Suppose You're Worth More Than You Think You Are (It's Time You Calculated Your Worth)

MATTHEW 9:9-13: As Jesus was walking along, he saw a man called Matthew sitting at the tax booth; and he said to him, "Follow me." And he got up and followed him.

And as he sat at dinner in the house, many tax collectors and sinners came and were sitting with him and his disciples. When the Pharisees saw this, they said to his disciples, "Why does your teacher eat with tax collectors and sinners?" But when he heard this, he said, "Those who are well have no need of a physician, but those who are sick. Go and learn what this means, 'I desire mercy, not sacrifice.' For I have come to call not the righteous but sinners."

Some people seem automatically to evoke the question, "What do you think they're worth?" Sometimes the question comes because of the house in which the family lives, the cars they drive, the clubs to which they belong. Sometimes, however, observers work from contrary data. They're sure some person is choosing to live below their means; gossip has it that they're "very comfortable."

I don't know in which category a man named Matthew fit. There's no hint as to whether he flaunted his wealth or whether he chose to live inauspiciously. I'm a little inclined to the former view. What we know for sure is that he was, as they say, well-fixed, so well-fixed that the people in his town speculated often about what he was worth. But I don't think Matthew himself thought much about it; or perhaps I should say, he thought about it only in a superficial way. He did, at least, until one day when everything in his life took a monumental turn.

Matthew was a tax collector. That phrase has the ring of civil service in our day, a position of trust and responsibility but not the sort of thing that leads to impressive wealth. But in the first-century Roman system, a tax collector was not a government employee but someone who had bought a franchise, like a Holiday Inn or McDonald's in our day. It seems the Roman government reasoned that since taxes were an unpleasant business, the best solution was to sell rights for the various taxing systems, and the owners of the franchises could then make as much money as the traffic would bear. Most of them did very well for themselves. After all (as we so often say), nothing in this world is certain but death and taxes, so a person who owns the right to collect taxes has a sure thing.

Now of course in a system like that, tax collectors never won any popularity contests. They couldn't say, "It's the government, you know"; the populace knew better. But what the tax collectors lost in general favor, they gained in fine houses, fine clothes, and often sumptuous living. In time, they won their own circle of friends. Between you and me, the circle tended to be a pretty motley crew, but friendship is a strange construct. Once you've accustomed yourself to another person's peculiarities and have found some reasonable areas of common interest, familiarity becomes comfort, and comfort passes for friendship. Matthew had friends, and he had a very comfortable life with security and promise.

It was that way, that is, until one day when a virtual stranger walked by, paused only long enough to catch Matthew's eye, and said, "Follow me." And Matthew rose up, left his business, his security, his future, and all of the common associations that make life enjoyable, and he followed the man.

You want more details? Matthew doesn't give us any more. As far as we know, the record we have is Matthew's own, and it is bare to the bone. Listen: "Jesus saw a man sitting at the tax collector's booth. 'Follow me,' he told him, and Matthew got up and followed him" (Matthew 9:9 NIV). This account is the closest thing we have to Matthew's own. It appears in the Gospel bearing his name, which suggests that the Gospel was written either by Matthew himself or by someone close enough to Matthew to dare to say that he was writing on Matthew's behalf. And the account Matthew gives is as matter-of-fact as if he were reporting what he ordered that day for lunch. He gives us no emotions, no color background.

Suppose you had been his wife, or his mother, or his older sibling, and Matthew had said that evening at the dinner table, "I left my business today."

"You mean you came home early? Come to think of it, I thought it was earlier than usual."

"No, I left my tax business."

"What do you mean?"

"Just what I said. I left my business today. The whole thing."

"You mean you sold it, sold your beautiful franchise?"

"No, I just left it."

"You didn't get anything for it? You just walked away?"

"Uh-huh."

"You must be out of your mind! Slowly, now, tell us exactly what happened."

"Well, this teacher came by. Jesus. I'd heard him sometimes, and so have you. He looked at me and said, 'Follow me,' so that's what I did. And that's what I'm going to do from now on. I'm going to follow him."

Isn't that a wild story? If someone in your family came home with such a report, you'd almost surely feel they'd been brainwashed. You'd want them to discuss it with some trusted friend or get an appointment with a psychiatrist or a counselor. And if you noticed that your family member seemed through it all to be utterly serene, you'd probably worry all the more.

So when you read the story, you can't help feeling there must be more to it. You want to know, as I do, what went through Matthew's mind, how much of a struggle he felt; you want to know something about the turmoil you're sure must have been going on in Matthew's soul.

Why didn't Matthew tell us these things? Perhaps it was modesty on Matthew's part. Perhaps he didn't want to glorify himself or make himself the center of the story. Or perhaps the story was just that simple, though I find it hard to think so.

Or perhaps this: Matthew told the story twenty, thirty years after it happened. Perhaps from the vantage point of the years, he saw how simple the decision was, how clear-cut the issues. Perhaps at the time when it actually happened, Matthew's soul was torn to the limits. It may be that as he tried to rise from his place to follow Jesus, he almost fainted under the struggle. He may have staggered as he first left his tax tables, grasping the side to brace himself as he followed on. It could have been that way; in fact, it seems reasonable that it was.

But as Matthew looked back on the matter, twenty or thirty years later, he may have seen how simple a choice it had been, or ought to have been. As he reconstructed the whole scene in his mind, he would picture the tax booth with its familiar books, records, and documents. He would remember the careful stacks of money, by denominations. It was all so familiar, so comfortable, so secure. But then he would also remember the sight of Jesus and the sound of his voice. Ah, he could never forget that! As he recalled it, nearly a generation later, perhaps it seemed to him that there was no struggle at all. How could there be a struggle when the choice was so clear-cut? Who could look at money and security then look at Jesus and wonder which was the better way? Thinking of it afterward, did Matthew remember another day when Jesus said, "What will it profit you if you gain the whole world and lose your soul?" (Matthew 16:26, para-phrase of KJV).

I wonder, then, twenty or thirty years after the event, if Matthew said to any who questioned him, "There wasn't really much to it. Jesus stopped and said, 'Follow me,' and I did. Do you think anything else mattered at that moment? What ever in the world *could* matter, compared to him?"

But if you know the rest of Matthew's story, you might wonder about Matthew making such a statement. This is because in the years that followed Matthew's decision, his life was often in danger because of his decision to follow Christ. He never knew the comfortable retirement on some Mediterranean beach that would have been his closing chapter if he had stayed with his franchise. At the end, he almost surely suffered a violent death. We have several traditions about the way he died, but all of them agree that he was a martyr and that his death was physically brutal. And of course he knew that it would probably end that way; at least, he knew so from the day he stood at a distance from a cross on Golgotha and watched Jesus die. He knew that if he continued to follow Jesus, his death, too, would no doubt be a dreadful one.

So how do we explain that day when a man left his profitable business and its security in order to respond to a passing voice? Strip away all the particulars, and it comes down to this: When Jesus said, "Follow me," Matthew had a chance to put his life in perspective. Indeed, the very call demanded that he do so. He had to ask himself, in whatever way he might put the question, *What am I worth? What do I amount to?*

On the one hand, he had a business, and a good one. It had its drawbacks, as all businesses and occupations do, but probably Matthew had gotten used to those factors. As for security, his business was all but guaranteed by what may well have been as secure a government as human history has known. Matthew could estimate his net worth in land, house, art objects, and investments, along with the prospects of future security, and the bottom line would look very, very good.

I'm not about to minimize this. I live in the same world you do. I have a retirement program and health insurance. I have a few investments, though I admit I don't pay any attention to them. If you were to take me into your confidence, to tell me your net worth and your plans for retirement, and perhaps to show me your home, your silver, your cars, and your boat, I would listen with empathy.

But then, after you had listed all these things, and perhaps all that you dream you might still get, I would want to ask, "Is that all you're worth? Is there anything here that will make the transition to eternity?" Because you know your house and boat and car and silver and mutual funds and retirement programs aren't negotiable in heaven—or in hell, either. So I ask, "Is that all you're worth? And is that all I'm worth?"

Which is to say: *Suppose you're worth more than you think you are.* Before Jesus stopped at Matthew's place of business, Matthew thought himself a businessman, a tax collector, and a man who was worth a fair piece of money. But Jesus put Matthew in new perspective. Matthew began to realize that *he was more than the sum total of his holdings.* Matthew realized he had a soul and that he was worth infinitely more than everything he owned or would ever be able to accumulate.

And so are you, and so am I. Whatever our holdings, whatever we've accumulated or hope to accumulate, we're worth more than that. Each year *Forbes* magazine lists the financial worth of the wealthiest persons. Some are identified as being worth thirty or forty billion dollars. But when I read such a report, I want to ask, "Is that all that man or woman is worth?" If so, feel sorry for them. Their price is inhumanely low.

So what do you do if you realize you're worth more than you've thought you were? In Matthew's case, he left his whole business, his measured security, to follow Jesus. I have no right to list the specifics of your response. Let me assure you that it isn't a matter of taking a call to the ministry. I'm afraid I've known people in my profession who are just as engrossed in materialism as the miser on the backstreet. No, a call to the ministry isn't the issue, because Christianity isn't enlistment in a profession.

But it is a matter of examining your value. I'm speaking not simply of your value as your accountant might know it; I want you to know that you're worth so much more than your house, your boat, your car, your jewels, your mutual funds, your pewter collection. You need to know that you're worth more than that. And knowing this, you need to begin living accordingly.

That is, you need to get a new bottom line for the decisions you make. Where once you made decisions on the basis of the bottom line of your economic worth, now you will make those decisions on the basis of your *eternal* worth. It's really that simple. Where once you asked, "How will this affect my retirement, or my holdings, or my economic security?" now—knowing what you're worth—you will ask, "How will this affect my soul, my eternal soul?"

When I was a young man, I had a brief business relationship with the father of a college student named Ed McCully. The father told me what a fine Christian his son was. A few years later that young man and four of his friends went to Ecuador to become missionaries to the Auca Indians, who until then had never heard the gospel. All five were killed by the very people they had hoped to save.

Some years before these young men and their families embarked on their missionary venture, one of them, Jim Elliot, had tried to think through what his life was worth. He summed his conclusion in a poignant sentence; after his death, his young widow included the sentence in the story of their heroic venture: "He is no fool who gives what he cannot keep to gain what he cannot lose" (Elisabeth Elliot, *Shadow of the Almighty: The Life and Testament of Jim Elliot* [New York: Harper & Brothers, 1958], p. 15).

I believe that's what Matthew realized. I think he looked at his business and all of the security it represented and said to himself, *Someday, as certain as the sun and moon, I will lose all of this. But Jesus! No one can ever take him from me. Not in time nor in eternity.*

That's what it means to find out what we're worth. And then, it's our business to live accordingly.

CHAPTER *10*

How Wide Is a Boat?
(Gladness Is Nearer Than You Think)

JOHN 21:1-12: After these things Jesus showed himself again to the disciples by the Sea of Tiberias; and he showed himself in this way. Gathered there together were Simon Peter, Thomas called the Twin, Nathanael of Cana in Galilee, the sons of Zebedee, and two others of his disciples. Simon Peter said to them, "I am going fishing." They said to him, "We will go with you." They went out and got into the boat, but that night they caught nothing.

Just after daybreak, Jesus stood on the beach; but the disciples did not know that it was Jesus. Jesus said to them, "Children, you have no fish, have you?" They answered him, "No." He said to them, "Cast the net to the right side of the boat, and you will find some." So they cast it, and now they were not able to haul it in because there were so many fish. That disciple whom Jesus loved said to Peter, "It is the Lord!" When Simon Peter heard that it was the Lord, he put on some clothes, for he was naked, and jumped into the sea. But the other disciples came in the boat, dragging the net full of fish, for they were not far from the land, only about a hundred yards off.

When they had gone ashore, they saw a charcoal fire there, with fish on it, and bread. Jesus said to them, "Bring some of the fish that you have just caught." So Simon Peter went aboard and hauled the net ashore, full of large fish, a hundred fifty-three of them; and though there were so many, the net was not torn. Jesus said to them, "Come and have breakfast." Now none of the disciples dared to ask him, "Who are you?" because they knew it was the Lord.

When I was in my midteens, I heard an evangelist named Charles S. Price. He was an old-fashioned orator with a flow of language we almost never hear in our day. Earlier in his career, he had been a lecturer with the Ellison-White Chautauqua circuit. In truth, I heard him every time I had a chance, even hitchhiking nearly a hundred miles to attend a camp meeting where he was preaching. I hung on his words, not only because he was a skilled speaker but also because I felt I had a call to preach, so I sought out every opportunity to hear outstanding preachers.

Each of his sermons moved me but none so much as the sermon "How Wide Is a Boat?" The sermon was built around an event in the last chapter of the Gospel of John. The events in the text occurred sometime after the Resurrection; John doesn't say exactly when. During those days following Easter, Jesus seems to have appeared at intervals, only to disappear without bidding farewell, then to appear again. I'm sure the disciples found this disconcerting. Of course they were profoundly moved by the Resurrection itself, but I'm equally sure they longed for things to be as they had been before the Crucifixion. That is, they wanted Jesus with them at all times; those had been the good old days, even if they hadn't always recognized it when it was the case. They couldn't help knowing that things had changed. It was increasingly clear that Jesus was no longer going to be their day-by-day physical possession. Perhaps they remembered that he had told them as much when he said that it was better for them that he go away so the Holy Spirit might come. But I think they found it hard to believe that they were better off without him; they much preferred his constant presence.

I'm sure their feelings fluctuated wildly during those days. At times, they probably felt ready to take the world captive for their Lord, but at other times they wondered why they had ever left the security of their boats and nets in order to follow a dream. I can't say what was in their minds on one of those evenings when seven of them came together, but it's easy to imagine. Simon Peter was there, of course; Thomas, Nathanael, James and John, and two others who are not named. Suddenly Peter, always the most verbal of the group, said, "I am going fishing." If one of us were to say this, we would be suggesting a break from the tedium or a setting for a different kind of conversation. But for Peter, I'm sure there was more to it. I suspect that when he said he was going fishing, it was his way of announcing that he might make a trial run at the world he knew best. Fishing wasn't recreation to Peter and his six companions; for at least Peter, James, and John, it had been their means of livelihood from their youth. They had left it behind in the wild, heady days when Jesus had first captured their souls. Now Peter, as I read him, was saying, "I'm going to see what it's like back in our old business."

Just as quickly the others said, "We will go with you." They had to be as anxious as Peter to get on with life. Whatever Jesus had meant to them (and it was much, no doubt of that), he was no longer going to be their daily companion. The dreams of his kingdom were now viewed most of the time through a haze of confusion. So they would go fishing. Fishing, they understood.

Only, they didn't. "They went out and got into the boat," the Gospel writer says, "but that night they caught nothing" (John 21:3). At first the boat must have felt very good. When you're surrounded by uncertainties, familiar objects are very welcome. A house you've known, the place you've worked, a familiar desk or computer station—they seem to exude strength because you've known them, and they're manageable. The tangled nets didn't so much frustrate as challenge. The evening was warm even though the sun was down. As they worked, the men threw their garments to the bottom of the boat so they could proceed unimpeded. They were basking in the masculine camaraderie, the pleasure of pitting their bodies against the elements of their work. They joked, I think, that after these years of just walking, talking, and learning, they weren't as strong as before. It was fun to feel pain in some long-forgotten muscles.

But still, they caught nothing. The excitement of a familiar role was beginning to tarnish a bit, as were their earlier jokes about having lost their touch as fishermen. They knew these waters so well; they could have mapped them for a marine biologist if there had been such. They knew not only where fish could be found but also what kind of fish at what time of the night. But not tonight. Again and again they threw down their nets, at first artfully, then desperately, and at last, frantically. And they caught nothing. Probably there are few human sensations more defeating than to let down a net and find no resistance when you draw it back. This is somehow worse than a farmer watching crops yield poorly or a salesperson getting a refusal. It's as if nature itself has set its powers against you.

So it's nearly morning, and they're slowly heading toward shore. Now they're in water that's probably too shallow to house a body of fish. Almost surely, they are defeated men. If their minds were like ours (and I suspect they were), the several strands of their lives now begin to interweave, so that one defeat simply adds color and texture to another. They had come to this familiar place with the questions of men who had followed a grand dream for three years (only now to wonder if the dream was never to be fulfilled in them) and had thought that here, in work that they knew so well, their egos would be restored. Instead, the very waters of home had become alien.

Just then there was a cry from the shore. "Children, you have no fish, have you?" (John 21:5). The voice and the greeting were so warm that they didn't think to be angered by the pain of the question. But their answer was without commentary, a simple "No." Now the stranger, in the mist of early morning, offered advice. "Cast the net to the right side of the boat, and you will find some" (John 21:6). People often marvel that the disciples listened to this counsel. They

were professionals. They knew their business. When Ted
Williams, the last batter to hit over .400, missed a strike (he
seldom did), did he listen patiently to some bleacher bum
who said, "Just pull up your left shoulder, Ted"? Does
Federal Reserve Chairman Alan Greenspan welcome email
counsel from the stranger who gets his economics from the
daily television news? When it came to fishing, why did the
disciples listen to the counsel of a stranger?

Perhaps they were so desperate that any idea seemed
worth a try. Or perhaps they sensed an authority in Jesus'
call that compelled them in spite of themselves. One wonders—the human mind being what it is—if perhaps, though
they didn't know it was Jesus, they caught the same eternal
inflection as had captured them three years before when
Jesus said, "Follow me." Whatever the reason, they did what
Jesus said. They cast their net on the other side of the boat.

Now, the Gospel writer tells us, their net was suddenly so
full that they couldn't pull it in. In that moment, John
shouted to Peter, "It is the Lord!" (John 21:7). We can only
speculate as to why John recognized Jesus. Most of our
Lord's resurrection appearances had about them an almost
surrealistic quality; in them, the people to whom he
appeared knew beyond a doubt that they were with Jesus,
but somehow he was also different, and they were never
sure how to deal with these anomalies. This is one of those
instances where the Gospel writer identifies John simply as
"that disciple whom Jesus loved"; I will dare to say that love's
perceptions are quicker than those of our physical senses.
John knew it was the Lord.

For Dr. Price, the rest of the story was anticlimactic. He
wanted to tell the congregation how near-at-hand were
hope, victory, and gladness. I can't recall, nearly two generations later, the specific ways the evangelist applied his point.
It's easy to imagine. Those were the years of the Great
Depression; Hitler and Mussolini were marching across
Europe, and the Far East (then a bit of a mystery to most of
us) was a complex of war and politics. But of course those

cataclysmic events were not the stuff of the evangelist's appeal that night. They formed a context of despair, but the people who heard the sermon were trying to cope with unpaid bills, landlords who wanted their rent, illnesses that threatened loved ones. And for all of these listeners, Dr. Price had a word: If they had been "fishing all night, and had caught nothing," hope was very near-at-hand. How near? Well, friend, how wide is a boat?

It was so simple. A cynical person would label it simplistic. Bills are still to be paid tomorrow, landlords to be reasoned with, unemployment lines to be maneuvered. What would change if one walked down the aisle to the altar of prayer?

I know the answer because I was there. I was a teenager, in a shirt Mother had made, trousers got with a slip from the County Relief Agency, socks that were mends upon mending. I was too smart for my neighborhood but without the proper clothing for the Latin class for which I had qualified. Several of my friends were poor, too, but not poor the way we were poor. I would read novels by William Heyliger and Ralph Henry Barbour about boys who went to prep school or to college; this was as much a fantasyland for me as was the comic strip "Buck Rogers in the 25th Century," but it was the world I dreamed of. But dreams or not, I knew that what Dr. Price said, about hope, was true. I knew that it wasn't far from my neighborhood, with all of its poverty and limitations, to the dreams of education and my call to the ministry.

How far? Well, how wide is a boat?

I have to tell you that there's more to the story. I had to throw my "nets" on the other side hundreds of times in the years between then and now. Very few of life's huge changes are complete in one act. But they do *begin* with one act. They begin with an act of faith in the One who asks if we've fished all night and caught nothing, an act so simple yet so profound as turning from the side of hopelessness to the side of hope.

So that night, after hearing that message, I walked home

singing. In the years since, all of the dreams of those years, and hundreds of dreams I wasn't equipped in those days to imagine, have been fulfilled. I've never stopped believing that, by the love of God in Christ, hope is near.

How near? Well, how wide is a boat?

CHAPTER 11

Strange Victory
(The Gains in Our Losses)

2 CORINTHIANS 12:1-10: It is necessary to boast; nothing is to be gained by it, but I will go on to visions and revelations of the Lord. I know a person in Christ who fourteen years ago was caught up to the third heaven—whether in the body or out of the body I do not know; God knows. And I know that such a person—whether in the body or out of the body I do not know; God knows—was caught up into Paradise and heard things that are not to be told, that no mortal is permitted to repeat. On behalf of such a one I will boast, but on my own behalf I will not boast, except of my weaknesses. But if I wish to boast, I will not be a fool, for I will be speaking the truth. But I refrain from it, so that no one may think better of me than what is seen in me or heard from me, even considering the exceptional character of the revelations. Therefore, to keep me from being too elated, a thorn was given me in the flesh, a messenger of Satan to torment me, to keep me from being too elated. Three times I appealed to the Lord about this, that it would leave me, but he said to me, "My grace is sufficient for you, for power is made perfect in weakness." So, I will boast all the more gladly of my weaknesses, so that the power of Christ may dwell in me. Therefore I am content with weaknesses, insults, hardships, persecutions, and calamities for the sake of Christ; for whenever I am weak, then I am strong.

I was a pastor for nearly forty years, so I've visited in literally thousands of homes. In more recent years, I have been the guest preacher in several hundred churches. In that experience, I've been in the offices of several hundred pastors and quite a few business and professional people as well. When you're in peoples' offices or homes, you quickly see what they're proud of. In a home, you'll usually see the pictures of family and close friends. In an office, the wall space is more often a collection of framed diplomas or documents giving evidence of professional standing. Sometimes a person also will have an autographed picture of some celebrity and occasionally a mounted newspaper article.

But in the thousands of homes and the hundreds of offices I've visited, I've never once seen a celebration of weakness or defeat. True, someone occasionally will display a booby prize from a golf tournament, just for the laughs; "a conversation piece," the owner says with peculiar pride. But no one mounts a newspaper story headlined "Local Businessman Declares Bankruptcy" or "Well-Known Couple Seeks Divorce." We don't plaster our walls with our defeats. To the contrary, we usually do everything we can to run from them and, if possible, to forget them; and certainly we do everything we can to divert the attention of others from such matters. We celebrate our victories and our achievements, not our weaknesses.

That's why we're not ready for a person who writes to a mixed group of his supporters and detractors, "If boasting there must be, I will boast of the things that show up my weakness" (2 Corinthians 11:30 REB). I don't suppose it will help much if I tell you that the person who wrote those words is someone who's now referred to as a saint. You're likely to say, "Well, of course saints are like that. They're an odd lot, you know. Nothing like us normal folks."

Actually, this man was very normal, and he wasn't given to needless self-disparagement. The truth be known, he was a very proud man. The line I've just quoted comes from a letter he wrote. A little earlier in the letter he gave in to some conventional boasting, talking about his family line and his professional achievements. Then he wrote at some length about the degree to which he had suffered in order to do his work, sounding something like an old soldier's war record or an athlete's list of breaks and bruises.

Then this man—the apostle Paul—does some more selective boasting, although in veiled fashion. If I were going to brag, he says, here's the kind of person I'd brag about. So he tells us about a man who had a supernatural experience fourteen years earlier. This man was "caught up into Paradise," where he heard things "that no mortal is permitted to repeat" (2 Corinthians 12:4). Paul says he would boast about someone like that, and of course the reader knows full well that Paul is talking about himself, that he is the person who has had this remarkable, mystical experience.

It's then that Paul levels with us. He says that because he had received such wonderful experiences, he was in danger of becoming "absurdly conceited" (2 Corinthians 12:7 JBP). So God did something special for him—special, but exceedingly strange. God gave him "a thorn ... in the flesh" (2 Corinthians 12:7).

Paul never tells us what this thorn in the flesh might be. Some people have speculated that it was his poor eyesight; it's likely Paul had an eye disease that was prevalent in the Middle East in those days, and we know that it was quite severe, since in another letter he refers to a "physical infirmity" and says that he knows "you would have torn out your eyes and given them to me" (Galatians 4:13, 15). Others think it could have been epilepsy, concluding from their studies that Paul may have been epileptic and that the affliction caused him both distress and shame, particularly in a culture that found negative spiritual connotations in certain illnesses. Others, projecting from things both said and unsaid, think the source of his pain was a bad marriage.

In truth, we don't know for sure, and we never will, short of eternity. But since Paul calls his problem a thorn in the flesh, it seems almost certain it was some kind of physical ailment. Very likely this was why he liked to have Luke, the beloved physician, as a traveling companion. A continuing affliction not only brought discomfort to Paul but also hindered him in his work.

Especially and ironically, his "thorn" had to be a peculiar kind of spiritual embarrassment. Paul was heralded on every side as a person of great faith. Others had such confidence in Paul's faith and piety that people sent handkerchiefs or aprons to the apostle, believing that if these items touched his body, healing would come to the afflicted (see Acts 19:12). How ironic, then, if Paul himself had a sickness from which he could get no relief! One imagines the whisperings that must at times have gone through the churches: "Strange, isn't it, that Paul can't get healed. What do you think is the impediment in his life?"

But we don't know what the thorn was. Paul did say that it was "a messenger of Satan to torment" him (2 Corinthians 12:7). That's pretty strong language! If Paul had identified his problem, I suspect people would ever thereafter have referred to it as "Paul's pain," the way we call the cartilage in the male throat the "Adam's apple." In our day, his thorn would probably be known as "the Pauline Syndrome." Besides, if Paul had so identified the problem or affliction, those in other generations who had such an ailment would attach special significance to it. As it is, any of us can read the story and relate to it in such a way that we get the greater truth Paul wants us to have, rather than being bogged down in incidental particulars.

No matter! The big truth is this, that Paul is *grateful* for his weakness. He has concluded that his weakness and his defeat are not dreadful, but wonderful. Paul tells us that three times he begged God to take this affliction from him, and that each time God refused. God said simply—perhaps rather abruptly and dismissively!—"My grace is enough for you: for where there is weakness, my power is shown the more completely" (2 Corinthians 12:9 JBP). And Paul says, "I'm happy with this arrangement." Actually, his language is much stronger than my paraphrase: "I can even enjoy weaknesses, insults, privations, persecutions and difficulties for Christ's sake" (2 Corinthians 12:10 JBP).

Paul has more to say, but let me stop right there, because I think that's where many of our contemporaries might stop. Our generation is likely to figure that Paul is really rather morbid. A person with good mental health, by our reasoning, doesn't wallow in defeat and in weakness. We want to say with Shakespeare's Hamlet that we choose "to take arms against a sea of troubles, / And by opposing end them." I think of William Ernest Henley, the nineteenth-century English poet and critic. A childhood bout with tuberculosis, which necessitated amputation of a foot when he was still a very young man, and a variety of other ills stirred him to issue a battle cry in his poem "Invictus":

> Out of the night that covers me,
>   Black as the pit from pole to pole,
> I thank whatever gods may be,
>   For my unconquerable soul.
> (*The World's Great Religious Poetry,* ed. Caroline
> Miles Hill [New York: Macmillan, 1923], pp. 588-89)

I like that! Something in me says that this is the way to respond to weakness and defeat: Shake your fist at "the fell clutch of circumstance," and march on with your head "bloody but unbowed" ("Invictus"). That appeals to me much more than what seems like a whimpering concession to defeat.

But in fact, Paul wasn't conceding defeat—the furthest thing from it. Rather, he was claiming a profound and wonderful victory. "Whenever I am weak," he wrote, "then I am strong" (2 Corinthians 12:10). Paul was satisfied at the core of his being that with his weakness, this stinging thorn in the flesh, he was a better, more able person than he was without it.

Let me make a significant distinction here. Many of us have been able to look back on some personal defeat or tragedy and say that it was all to the good. We may even say that it was one of the best things that ever happened to us. But this is usually after such a defeat is history. Paul isn't talking history, he's talking right now. The thorn is still with him, still to be coped with day and night. He expects that he will always have to deal with it. And he's *glad.* He's thankful—not for weakness past, but for weakness present, and most likely, future.

Why? Because Paul has found that it is this very weakness that makes him strong in Christ. Take away this weakness, and he is a better-than-average preacher and teacher with a fine mind, a superb education, and a fair degree of arrogance. And that, as we say, is not just chopped liver. True. But it doesn't compare with what Paul is when he is *weak.* Because when Paul is weak, he becomes a uniquely effective conduit for the grace and power of God.

So Paul isn't putting on a pious act, nor is he being heroic or wonderfully idealistic when he rejoices in his weakness. He's being very tough-minded and realistic about himself and about life. He has looked at the bottom line of his life: what kind of person he was without his weakness and what kind of person he now is with this weakness. The conclusion is obvious. He is simply much better, much more productive, much more winsome and Christlike. He is a bigger, better, more well-rounded human being. No wonder, then, that he looks at his weakness and says, "I'll keep it." Of course!

Rhoda Blecker has come to handle her weakness with a grin. Our generation, at least in the Western world, puts huge store by physical attractiveness. Everybody is supposed to be *beautiful!* Rhoda observes that she has been blessed with many things and that, if she were beautiful too, she "would have fallen into arrogance, thoughtlessness and selfishness." So, she concludes, she's grateful that God "knew what He was doing when He decided to give me a roundish body, a narrow forehead and pouchy eyes. He knew I'd need them to find my way from myself and closer to Him" (*Daily Guideposts*, 2001 [Carmel, N.Y.: Guideposts, 2000], p. 187).

I speak from experience. I've had some small successes in my life. Enough, at least, to evoke occasional envy and enough to satisfy the ambitions of a boy who grew up in the wrong neighborhood but who believed he could compete in the next neighborhood. God has blessed me with a reasonably good mind; I can write some, and I can preach some.

But gradually I have come to realize that my most important possession is a weakness. I have an inordinate capacity for regret. As it happens, I've done enough that is wrong, and have made enough mistakes, and have hurt enough people—even if usually unintentionally—to have ample reason for regret. Nevertheless, people with good mental health learn how to put their failures in perspective. Tennyson spoke of being "wild with all regret"; I understand that feeling. And as if big and real regrets are not enough, I'm a specialist in turning minor matters into substantial regrets. If someone waves while driving by and I fail to see their greeting in time to return it, I can regret it well into next week. Sometimes it will even reappear on the screen of my memory several years later. So not only do I have enough major reasons for legitimate regret but also intricate skill in inventing minor ones, as if I'm dedicated to keeping myself continually in good supply.

Regret isn't by any means a totally bad thing. As a matter of fact, it can make us change our ways and strive to be better. But then we ought to be done with it. That's what I can't do. I know I'm forgiven, because I know what the Bible says about these things. And when possible, I seek to make amends. But some regrets have stayed with me for much of my life, and I have transient ones each week. So I understand the pathology of regret, and if you come to me with your regrets, I can help you find the way out. Like Paul, I can be a channel of healing for others, while my own sickness remains.

But I've learned that this weakness of mine is my special strength. Without it, I would be quite insufferable. With it, I am driven daily to rely on Christ and to order my conduct with care. So I thank God for my wonderful weakness. It gives me pain every day, but it blesses me beyond measure. I rejoice in my strange victory.

Many people are brought to God by trouble. Even more of us are kept close to God by our weakness. This isn't the way we'd like it to be. We'd rather say with William Ernest Henley, "I am the master of my fate, / I am the captain of my soul" ("Invictus"). But in truth, some weakness that we despise may be our greatest strength. So remember, anything that draws us closer to God, or *keeps* us close to him, and that helps us to grow in character is a supreme gift.

During most of the apostle Paul's adult life, he really didn't have a home. He traveled from city to city, preaching the gospel, beginning churches, testifying to his faith. Sometimes he stayed in the homes of others; sometimes he was in prison, sometimes in rented quarters. But I doubt that he ever had a place—a home or an office—where he could put up his mementos: his graduation certificate, his membership in the Pharisees, some written testimonials to his greatness. He had no place to post such items.

But if he had, I know what Paul would have hung on the wall of his home or office. It would be evidence, in some form, of his thorn in the flesh, whatever it was. Perhaps a hate letter—heaven knows he got them!—or maybe a reminder of his argument with Barnabas, evidences of his weakness. And if you had said to him, "Don't those pictures and mementos embarrass you? Don't they depress you?" I think Paul would answer, "Oh, no! These are the things that make me strong. They keep me close to Christ. I really couldn't survive without them. They're beautiful, wonderful. They're my weaknesses. They're a continuing miracle in my life."

CHAPTER 12

The View from Mount Nebo
(And Then, There Is Heaven)

DEUTERONOMY 34:1-8: Then Moses went up from the plains of Moab to Mount Nebo, to the top of Pisgah, which is opposite Jericho, and the LORD showed him the whole land: Gilead as far as Dan, all Naphtali, the land of Ephraim and Manasseh, all the land of Judah as far as the Western Sea, the Negeb, and the Plain—that is, the valley of Jericho, the city of palm trees—as far as Zoar. The LORD said to him, "This is the land of which I swore to Abraham, to Isaac, and to Jacob, saying, 'I will give it to your descendants'; I have let you see it with your eyes, but you shall not cross over there." Then Moses, the servant of the LORD, died there in the land of Moab, at the LORD's command. He was buried in a valley in the land of Moab, opposite Beth-peor, but no one knows his burial place to this day. Moses was one hundred twenty years old when he died; his sight was unimpaired and his vigor had not abated. The Israelites wept for Moses in the plains of Moab thirty days; then the period of mourning for Moses was ended.

W hen you're a pastor, people sometimes come to you with questions you can't answer. I'm not speaking of textbook replies, or superficial little truisms. That kind of answer isn't hard to give, nor does it serve much purpose after it's given. I'm speaking of those instances where people are dealing with some pain that cannot really be removed, and they bring the pain to you.

A woman came to me who had gone through a divorce several years before. It had not been a hasty act; she had searched and struggled for other solutions, but without success, until at last she had taken a course that went against every fiber of her being: a divorce. Subsequent events had proved that her decision had been the right one—right, in the sense of being inevitable—but now she was looking at some of the fallout. She explained to me that she was sentimental, so she had always dreamed what it would be like when her children married—the weddings, the enlarged family, the grandchildren. Now, divorced, she was contemplating the complications that had taken over her dreams. With a divided family, what had once been dream occasions sounded more like ordeals to be endured.

As she looked back on her life, she noted that a person makes some mistakes that bring consequences that can't be changed. The mistakes can be explained and understood and the sins forgiven. But the consequences remain. We have to live with the consequences.

I understood what she was saying, and if you have lived for even a few years, you understand too. I couldn't give her a pretty little formula. I could only tell her the story of Moses. And I was glad, glad I could lead her up Mount Nebo.

Moses was an extraordinary human being, legendary in his dimensions. Some cultures remember him as one of the premier lawgivers of human history. The Jews remember him for that but even more for his role as a pioneer of freedom. Those of us who have read our Bibles with some care recall that he was a person so trusted by God that he would dare to challenge what he perceived to be God's judgments and a person who desired God so much that he dared to ask God if he might see the divine face (see Exodus 32:7-14; 33:12-23).

But with all of that, Moses was very human. I don't know how many mistakes he made in his life. The Bible records several, and I suspect that, being human, he had many more. One of those mistakes was of such crucial dimensions that he paid for it to the day of his death. Some mistakes and some sins are like that. And I hasten also to say that some of the things that happen to us, things outside our control, things that are not our mistakes but that are forced on us by circumstances or by other people, are like that. Most of life's experiences are of such a kind that we can redeem part of what is lost and, in some instances, gain more than was lost. But some of our human errors and sins and some of the events that come our way can never fully be remedied on this earth.

Moses' experience came at a bad time. Of course that makes sense because it's at bad times that we're likely to lose control and to do the wrong thing. Even Moses' normal experiences were distressing enough because his people, the Israelites, were as difficult and unappreciative a congregation as any leader has ever been called to serve. This wasn't entirely their fault; they didn't have much going for them when Moses took over the helm. No matter, they were difficult. And sometimes Moses' prime associate, his brother Aaron, wasn't that helpful either. Take the time that Moses was on Mount Sinai, getting a sermon of such significance that it was engraved in stone. When he got back from his study retreat, he found that Aaron had transferred the whole blessed congregation to another denomination, so to speak, and an exceedingly questionable one at that (see Exodus 32:1-6, 19-24).

Within a short time Moses went through the debacle of sending a committee of twelve to spy out the land toward which they were marching, their long-hoped-for promised land, and the committee brought back a report that caused a rebellion among the people (see Numbers 13–14:10*a*); then there was an uprising under Korah, Dathan, and Abiram (Numbers 16); and then, at Kadesh, Moses' sister, Miriam, died (Numbers 20:1). I'm sure that was particularly upsetting. After all, she was the big sister who had watched over Moses in his infancy at the Nile River. Without a doubt, Moses felt this loss.

Then it happened. Israel ran out of water again. Of course they blamed their predicament on Moses. Moses learned, long before Harry Truman made the phrase famous, that the buck stops with the leader. As with all their crises, the people got hysterical, and, with the peculiar sort of memory that comes at such times, they began to recall all the grievances they had ever known. "Why did you bring us up out of Egypt to this terrible place?" they asked. "It has no grain or figs, grapevines or pomegranates" (Numbers 20:5 NIV). The people of Israel were always complaining about the menu; somehow they reasoned that they should always find a delicatessen at the corners of Kadesh and Barnea. But worst of all—and this was a very legitimate gripe—there was no water to drink.

So Moses and Aaron came into the presence of God, where they fell flat on their faces, and the glory of the Lord appeared to them. God told Moses that the two of them, Moses and Aaron, should gather the people together and that they should speak to a rock, and it would pour out its water.

But Moses was upset. You can tell this by the way he addressed the congregation. "Listen, you rebels," he said. When a spiritual leader calls the congregation rebels or hypocrites or dummies, you know that he or she is upset. And for that matter, if the pastor calls them "beloved" but says it with a snarl, well, you know there's trouble on the way. "Listen, you rebels," he said, "must we bring you water out of this rock?" And with that, Moses raised his arm and struck the rock with his staff. Struck it twice, in fact. Sure enough, water gushed out (Numbers 20:10-11 NIV).

The people were satisfied, and Moses no doubt felt pretty good too. But God wasn't happy. God said, "Because you did not trust in me enough to honor me as holy in the sight of the Israelites, you will not bring this community into the land I give them" (Numbers 20:12 NIV).

It's hard to define Moses' sin exactly. Certainly there was disobedience. He had been told to *speak* to the rock, and instead he struck it, twice. That's bad enough because disobedience is, after all, the basic sin. And Moses was *angry,* as I have indicated. Now there's such a thing as being angry for the Lord, but it's also possible (especially for a preacher) to be angry because you feel people haven't given you proper respect. Still worse, it sounds as if Moses was taking some of the glory of God to himself. "Must we bring you water out of this rock?" he cried—almost as if he had something to do with the miracle besides saying the words he'd been told to say. Those of us who serve Christ are always susceptible to this confusion of authority and power, but most of us don't get such a dramatic instance as did Moses.

God's answer to Moses and Aaron was short and direct. "Because you did not trust in me enough to honor me as holy in the sight of the Israelites, you will not bring this community into the land I give them." We might think hard about this matter of honoring God as holy in the sight of people. It's an area of temptation for any of us who do a kind or worthy thing out of holy impulse, then accept the praise as if we were persons of unusual merit.

So the day came, years later, when Moses was to die. And God said, "Go to Mount Nebo, across from Jericho, and view Canaan" (Deuteronomy 32:49, paraphrase). Moses wouldn't get to enter the promised land, but he would get a view of it from Mount Nebo. Thank God for the view from Mount Nebo!

I love to speak the hopeful word. I find it difficult to speak a word of final loss because I find it hard to think there's no more hope. But I have to confess that some things in this life get broken—especially, some that *we* break!—that cannot be repaired in this life. Moses learned as much. He recovered from most of his mistakes and probably used them to become a better and more able person. But not so with what he did at Meribah. Here was a mistake that shut him out of the promised land. As he neared the end of his life-journey, he must have said, a thousand times over, "Why did I strike that rock? How could I have been so stupid, so arrogant, so dull of reason?" And I wonder if sometimes he begged God; I wonder if he asked, "Couldn't I go there for just a day? Maybe just a weekend excursion?"

But it wasn't to be so. Some things that are broken can't be put together again. Not on this earth. By some acts, we shut ourselves out of some promised lands. Mind you, by the grace of God we're often able to find a happy substitute. And it is sublimely true that "in everything God works for good with those who love him" (Romans 8:28 RSV) so that we seem sometimes to come out better than under the old plan. No matter, all of us come to some waters of Meribah, where we miss God and where we strike the rock when we shouldn't; and by doing so, we close the door to some promised land.

But sometimes the broken thing is not of our own doing. Sometimes life itself seems to crumble to pieces in our hands, and we can't do anything about it. In other generations, parents who lost a child during infancy sometimes gave another child the same name. My grandparents named their first born Wilhelm, after his father. But when the boy was only eight, he died. Eight years later, they named another son Wilhelm. He carried on the cherished family name, but I'm altogether sure he didn't take the place of his first-born sibling. Not really. My grandparents could have named a dozen boys Wilhelm, but they would still miss the eight-year-old they lost.

Is there any grace at such a time? When the portion of the promised land named Elizabeth is no longer a possibility, is there any hope, any grace? Just this, for sure: You can go up on Mount Nebo, and you can view the land from there. There is a magnificent view from Mount Nebo.

In 1986 I gave the baccalaureate sermon at Asbury Theological Seminary. A young man from that graduating class had been killed in an automobile accident the previous winter. The seminary did a lovely thing: They brought his parents to the commencement ceremony, and just before the diplomas were distributed, the parents were called to the platform to receive a special document in recognition of their son's anticipated graduation. I watched them with pain, praying for them, wondering how one could relieve their hurt. A few moments later, as the members of the graduating class began walking across the stage to receive their diplomas, the mother and father quietly rose from their seats and left the auditorium. I'm sure they realized they couldn't endure the pain of watching their son's classmates walk across the platform while their boy was buried on some hillside. They would never enter this particular promised land with their son. Take them, please, to Mount Nebo!

People sang so many songs about heaven when I was growing up. I remember especially a song that went like this:

> We are often destitute
> of the things that life demands,
> want of food and want of shelter,
> thirsty hills and barren lands;
> we are trusting in the Lord,
> and according to God's Word,
> we will understand it better by and by.
> (Charles Albert Tindley, "We'll Understand It
> Better By and By," *The United Methodist Hymnal*
> [Nashville: The United Methodist Publishing
> House, 1989], p. 525)

I remember how often people cried as they sang that hymn, and how some would lift their faces heavenward and close their eyes as they sang the refrain:

> By and by, when the morning comes,
> when the saints of God are gathered home,
> we'll tell the story how we've overcome,
> for we'll understand it better by and by.

Now I know why they cried: because the song was leading them up to the top of Mount Nebo, and the view was good from Mount Nebo.

A generation or more ago, a certain breed of scholar got hold of a phrase that mocked belief in the world to come. They said it was pie-in-the-sky-when-you-die-by-and-by religion. I submit that they said this sort of thing because they didn't get close enough to the pain to approach Mount Nebo. Jonathan Kozol is a Harvard graduate, an outstanding scholar, and a penetrating writer. As a fearless student of the contemporary scene, he deals in hard facts, and he handles those facts with tough logic. But when he moved into the ghetto of New York City's South Bronx in the 1990s to see what was happening to the children there, something happened to him. He said that he cried for two years while writing his book *Amazing Grace: The Lives of Children and the Conscience of a Nation.*

And something more happened. During those days, to his own surprise, he started reading the Bible again. "I found I was thinking of heaven all the time," he said. "I long to believe there is a heaven because it seems unbearable that the children I met won't have something wonderful for them after they die. The lives we give them in America aren't enough to justify existence" (Anita Manning, "When Society Fails, Children Suffer," *USA Today,* Tuesday, October 24, 1995).

I don't know that Mr. Kozol would say it this way, but he's going up to the top of Mount Nebo. He is working passionately, with the voice and energy of an Old Testament prophet, to bring change—in law, in social conscience, in education. But for some of the children it is already too late; there is no promised land for them in the South Bronx. Kozol has been driven to seek a view from Mount Nebo.

This is the word I must speak, preaching and living as I do in a fallen world. Sometimes because we have ourselves made wrong decisions and have struck a rock when we shouldn't have, we lose some piece of earth's promised land, and sometimes by the cruelty of others or by the sheer irrationality of life and nature, we lose some things that can never be regained on this earth. They're gone; that's it. Sometimes there is no second chance, no alternative, no medical miracle.

At such times the facts tell me that life on this earth is not necessarily fair. But faith tells me that there is heaven. I believe in heaven. I believe in it because the Bible tells me so. I also believe in heaven because my heart insists on it. And my heart has such an insistence because some prior reality has laid hold of my heart; a piece of heaven has laid primeval claim there. So when I see a place where all the doors on this earth are closed, I walk by faith to the top of Mount Nebo. From there, the view is good. It can be trusted.

Life from the
Up Side

JOHN D. SCHROEDER

T his book by J. Ellsworth Kalas takes a fresh look at stories from the Bible and applies their lessons to life today. To assist you in facilitating a discussion group, this study guide was created to help make this experience beneficial for both you and members of your group. Here are some thoughts on how you can help your group.

SUGGESTIONS FOR LEADERS

1. Distribute the book to participants before your first meeting and request that they come having read the brief introduction and the first chapter. You may want to limit the size of your group to increase participation.

2. Begin your sessions on time. Your participants will appreciate your promptness. You may wish to begin your first session with introductions and a brief get-acquainted time. Start each session by reading aloud the snapshot summary of the chapter for the day.

3. Select discussion questions and activities in advance. Note that the first question is a general question designed to get discussion going. The last question is designed to summarize the discussion. Feel free to change the order of the listed questions and to create your own questions. Allow a set amount of time for the questions and activities.

4. Remind your participants that all questions are valid as part of the learning process. Encourage their participation in discussion by saying that there are no "wrong" answers and that all input will be appreciated. Invite participants to share their thoughts, personal stories, and ideas as their comfort level allows.

5. Some questions may be more difficult to answer than others. If you ask a question and no one responds, begin the discussion by venturing an answer yourself. Then ask for comments and other answers. Remember that some questions may have multiple answers.

6. Ask the question "Why?" or "Why do you believe that?" to help continue a discussion and give it greater depth.

7. Give everyone a chance to talk. Keep the conversation moving. Occasionally you may want to direct a question to a specific person who has been quiet. "Do you have anything to add?" is a good follow-up question to ask another person. If the topic of conversation gets off track, move ahead by asking the next question in your study guide.

8. Before moving from questions to activities, ask group members if they have any questions that have not been answered. Remember that, as a leader, you do not have to know all the answers. Some answers may come from group members. Other answers may even need a bit of research. Your job is to keep the discussion moving and to encourage participation.

9. Review the activity in advance. Feel free to modify it or to create your own activity. Encourage participants to try the "At home" activity.

10. Following the conclusion of the activity, close with a brief prayer, praying either the printed prayer from the study guide or a prayer of your own. If your group desires, pause for individual prayer petitions.

11. Be grateful and supportive. Thank group members for their ideas and participation.

12. You are not expected to be a "perfect" leader. Just do the best you can by focusing on the participants and the lesson. God will help you lead this group.

13. Enjoy your time together!

SUGGESTIONS FOR PARTICIPANTS

1. What you will receive from this study will be in direct proportion to your involvement. Be an active participant!

2. Please make a point to attend all sessions and to arrive on time so that you can receive the greatest benefit.

3. Read the chapter and review the questions in the study guide prior to the meeting. You may want to jot down questions you have from the reading and also answers to some of the questions from the study guide.

4. Be supportive and appreciative of your group leader as well as the other members of your group. You are on a journey together.

5. Your participation is encouraged. Feel free to share your thoughts about the material being discussed.

6. Pray for your group and your leader.

CHAPTER 1

On Being Born with a Rusty Spoon
(For Those Who've Had a Bad Start)

SNAPSHOT SUMMARY

This chapter shows how "a bad start" in life does not have to limit our potential for serving God.

REFLECTION / DISCUSSION QUESTIONS

1. Explain what it means that each of us was born with a rusty spoon.
2. Reflect on / discuss some of the unpleasant realities of life that seem to suggest that "we are born into a world where sin was here before we were."
3. In what ways are we directly shaped by the generations that have come before us?
4. Why do you think the spies selected the house of Rahab as a hideout?
5. How is the story of Rahab a rusty-spoon story?
6. Reflect on / discuss what happened to Rahab after Israel conquered Jericho.
7. How is Rahab an example of faith and works?
8. What lessons about God did you learn from the story of Rahab?
9. Share an example of how you or someone you know overcame difficult situations or circumstances through faith.
10. What new insights did you receive from reading this chapter?

ACTIVITIES

As a group: Make a list of things or circumstances in life that can limit us or hold us back. Then make a list of things that help us overcome our difficulties or challenges.

At home: Look at what you have "inherited," and ponder how you can use it to accomplish God's purpose for your life.

Prayer: Dear God, thank you for giving us no limits in our potential for serving you, no matter how we start out in life. Help us to learn from the example of Rahab and to respond constructively to the challenges we face while always maintaining our faith in you. Thank you for always being with us. Amen.

CHAPTER 2
When Life is at January (Who Knows What Wonders Lie Ahead?)

SNAPSHOT SUMMARY

This chapter examines beginnings that are not always so neat and tidy.

REFLECTION / DISCUSSION QUESTIONS

1. What choices are *not* ours to make in life?
2. How does it feel to be thrust into something without a choice?
3. Reflect on / discuss what you like or dislike about the month of January.
4. How is the Genesis story a January story?
5. Share a time when you learned that beginnings are not easy.
6. What is the importance of genealogy in Genesis?
7. What message does the story of Abraham have for us today?

8. How do you usually respond when there are challenging circumstances or events that are beyond your control?

9. What unexpected events occur in the Genesis stories mentioned in the chapter?

10. Why is it wise to expect the unexpected?

ACTIVITIES

As a group: Reflect on / discuss what God expects from us when life is at January, that is, when life doesn't seem to be going anywhere or when we find ourselves at an uncertain beginning.

At home: Open your eyes this week to see the unexpected and to see the new paths where God is leading you. Ponder what wonders lie ahead.

Prayer: Dear God, thank you for life's unexpected surprises. Help us to remember that while we don't know what the future holds, we do know that you and your love are constant. May we make the most of the talents and opportunities you provide to us. Amen.

CHAPTER 3

A Woman Who Lived with Scorn
(For Those Who Suffer Rejection
Close at Hand)

SNAPSHOT SUMMARY

This chapter examines the consequences of rejection and indifference.

REFLECTION / DISCUSSION QUESTIONS

1. Share how scorn has touched your life.

2. Reflect on / discuss the importance physical attractiveness plays in our society. What advantages do attractive people have?

3. List some reasons why people are scorned.

4. In what ways were Leah and Rachel different? How do you think they felt about each other?

5. Why did Jacob love Rachel more than he did Leah?

6. Who do you think loved Jacob more, Leah or Rachel? Explain your answer.

7. Do you think that Leah thought Jacob would grow to love her? Explain.

8. What toll does it take on a person who is repeatedly scorned?

9. How does God feel about those who scorn others?

10. What do you think motivates people to scorn? What should we do as individuals and as a society to treat others with love and respect?

ACTIVITIES

As a group: Pretend you are Jacob. If you were in his shoes, what would you have done regarding relationships with Leah and Rachel?

At home: Examine your life this week for any indifference or rejection of others. Reflect on treating others as you wish to be treated.

Prayer: Dear God, thank you for accepting us and loving us just as we are. You love each one of us in equal measure, even though we are all different. Help us to treat others as we wish to be treated. Open our eyes to what we have in common with others. Close our eyes to differences. Amen.

CHAPTER 4
Don't Blame the Donkey!
(Capitalize on Your Adversity)

SNAPSHOT SUMMARY

This chapter offers encouragement to learn from life's experiences.

REFLECTION / DISCUSSION QUESTIONS

1. Reflect on / discuss why experience is such a good teacher. Share something you learned from experience.

2. List and reflect on / discuss reasons we fail to learn from experience.

3. Why did Balaam get angry at the donkey?

4. What blinded Balaam to the reason for the donkey's behavior? How might Balaam have responded differently in this situation?

5. What causes people to be poor students? List some reasons.

6. Why do students often fail to recognize their teachers in the School of Experience?

7. Reflect on / discuss why we often fail to learn from success.

8. The author says that "the process of learning always requires a certain measure of humility." What else facilitates learning?

9. Why is it that we curse at our circumstances instead of learning from them?

10. What other lessons can we learn from the story of Balaam and his donkey?

ACTIVITIES

As a group: Make a list of and reflect on / discuss some of the teachers in the School of Experience, including Love, Friendship, and Defeat. Name some other teachers.

At home: Reflect on what you have learned so far in life and how you have been taught life's lessons.

Prayer: Dear God, thank you for giving us the opportunity to learn from our experiences. Help us to be good students and to grow in our faith. May we also learn to love and help others. Amen.

CHAPTER 5
When You've Been Given a Bad Name (Don't Let Others Define You)

SNAPSHOT SUMMARY

This chapter provides encouragement for overcoming labels others place upon us.

REFLECTION / DISCUSSION QUESTIONS

1. Share what you know about your name: What is its meaning? Who, if anyone, are you named after, and why?
2. What was it like for you growing up with your name?
3. What is known about Eli, the judge?
4. List and reflect on / discuss the tragedies in the story of Eli (particularly regarding the battle and the birth).
5. How did the sons of Eli try to manipulate God?
6. For what reasons did Phinehas's wife name her child Ichabod?

7. Why are names important?

8. List and reflect on / discuss some negative names or labels that people are given by society or even by family.

9. Why is the name we give ourselves more important than all others?

10. Reflect on / discuss how you can "change" your name.

ACTIVITIES

As a group: Reflect on / discuss some strategies for rising above a name.

At home: Think about the distinct character of names. Locate a book or other source about the meaning of different names and look for information about the names of people in your life.

Prayer: Dear God, thank you for calling us each by name. Open our eyes to the good in others and help us not to place labels upon people. May we grow in love toward you and in friendship toward one another. Amen.

CHAPTER 6
Color Her Moses
(Never Give Up. Never.)

SNAPSHOT SUMMARY

This chapter encourages us not to give up, even when God seems silent.

REFLECTION / DISCUSSION QUESTIONS

1. In what ways was the Canaanite woman like Moses?
2. How did the disciples react to the woman?

3. Why did Jesus treat the Canaanite woman as he did?

4. What do you admire about the Canaanite woman?

5. Share a time in your life when God seemed to be silent.

6. What can you do when God is silent? Is silence sometimes an answer? Explain.

7. How and why did Moses argue with God? What was the outcome? (See Exodus 32:7-14.)

8. What lessons are there in the story of Jesus and the Canaanite woman?

9. Do you think God answers some prayers but not others? Explain your answer.

10. What sometimes happens when we must wait or struggle with an answer to prayer?

ACTIVITIES

As a group: List and reflect on / discuss the different ways in which God answers prayer. Why can persistence be important?

At home: Reflect on your unanswered prayers. Talk to God about your requests and your reasons for asking.

Prayer: Dear God, thank you for letting us come to you at any time just to talk or to ask for help. You are always there, and you're always listening. Help us to be patient and persistent when we need to be. Above all, help us to remember that you love us. Amen.

CHAPTER 7
Plot for a Life (More Than Success)

SNAPSHOT SUMMARY

This chapter shows how Jesus gives life meaning, gives it a plot.

REFLECTION / DISCUSSION QUESTIONS

1. What do we know about Bartimaeus? How do we know that he was not born blind?

2. What impresses you about the story of Jesus healing Bartimaeus?

3. Why was Bartimaeus "without a plot" until he met Jesus?

4. Share your views and opinions about life.

5. Do you believe there is a grand story in every person's life just waiting to happen? Explain your thoughts.

6. Compare and contrast life with and without Jesus.

7. What role does faith play in the course of our lives?

8. How did Mother Teresa give dying people a plot?

9. Explain why having a plot means more than being successful.

10. What does it mean that we are eternal beings?

ACTIVITIES

As a group: Use your Bible to locate people who gained a plot after meeting Jesus. Compare their life before and after meeting Jesus.

At home: Take a walk to a place where you can collect your thoughts and meditate on life.

Prayer: Dear God, thank you for creating us as eternal beings who can love you now and forever. Help us to focus on what is important in life. May we continue to receive your healing touch upon our spirit as we serve you and others on this earth. Amen.

CHAPTER 8
Party Gone Flat
(What to Do When Life Loses Its Flavor)

SNAPSHOT SUMMARY

This chapter shows how God cares about ordinary people and their everyday needs and how Jesus brings zest to life.

REFLECTION / DISCUSSION QUESTIONS

1. Why would it have been considered a disaster for the wedding hosts to run out of wine?
2. Why do you think Jesus changed the water into wine?
3. How did this miracle change the disciples' view of Jesus?
4. Why do you think Mary insisted on Jesus solving the problem?
5. How are weddings used in the Bible as a symbol? List some of the things a wedding represents.
6. In what ways was this miracle also a sign?
7. Reflect on / discuss the ways in which Jesus brings continual excitement to life.
8. How do you define a miracle? Have you ever experienced one? If so, share some details about it.
9. What lessons about God and our relationship with God can we learn from this Bible passage?
10. What other insights did you gain from reading this chapter?

ACTIVITIES

As a group: Share examples of life gone flat; use a newspaper, magazine, or other sources to locate examples.

At home: Reflect on your life and how much more Jesus can add to it if you will let him.

Prayer: Dear God, thank you for the excitement you add to life. Open our hearts and minds to giving you a larger role in our lives. Help us not to settle for a life that is flat but to live out our Christian faith with all the joy and zest that you intend for us. Amen.

CHAPTER 9

Suppose You're Worth More Than You Think You Are
(It's Time You Calculated Your Worth)

SNAPSHOT SUMMARY

This chapter compares your economic worth to your eternal worth.

REFLECTION / DISCUSSION QUESTIONS

1. What was Matthew's life like as a tax collector? What was he lacking?

2. Speculate on the reasons why Matthew gave up everything to follow Jesus.

3. In what ways are you like Matthew before he became a follower of Jesus?

4. Why is it that people often base their personal value on their income and possessions?

5. How are you changed when you discover your eternal worth?

6. What makes it so easy to focus on wealth and forget about our eternal worth?

7. Share a time when you gave up your security. What were your reasons for doing so? What was the outcome?

8. What does it take to put your whole life into perspective? Explain.

9. How are you worth more than you think you are? Explain your answer.

10. What new insights have you gained about your real worth from reading this chapter?

ACTIVITIES

As a group: Reflect on / discuss what it means to know your eternal value and to live accordingly.

At home: Make a list of what you cannot keep. Make a second list of what is eternally yours.

Prayer: Dear God, thank you for the high value you place on every one of us. Make us always mindful of what is important in life and what is not. Help us value our friends and our family; and may we value our relationship with you, through your son Jesus Christ, above everything else. Amen.

CHAPTER 10
How Wide Is a Boat?
(Gladness Is Nearer Than You Think)

SNAPSHOT SUMMARY

This chapter shows how an act of faith can mean the difference between hope and hopelessness.

REFLECTION / DISCUSSION QUESTIONS

1. What questions and doubts did the disciples have after the Resurrection?

2. Reflect on / discuss the reasons the disciples may have decided to go fishing.

3. What must have been the mood of the disciples after catching no fish?

4. Reflect on / discuss why the disciples listened to the advice from the stranger on the shore.

5. According to the author, for what reason might John have recognized the stranger as Jesus?

6. As the author describes it, what was Dr. Price's message of hope?

7. Share a time when you were struggling and needed hope. How did it feel?

8. Share a time when gladness was closer than it seemed.

9. What's the difference between hopelessness and hope?

10. What other lessons can we learn from this chapter?

ACTIVITIES

As a group: Reflect on / discuss acts of hope and faith that are happening in our world today.

At home: Meditate on a challenge you are facing. Consider how your faith can help you meet that challenge.

Prayer: Dear God, thank you for hope and faith, two of the most powerful forces in this world. Help us to remember that we can always call on you in times of trouble. May we remember that you and your love are always with us, now and through eternity. Amen.

CHAPTER 11
Strange Victory
(The Gains in Our Losses)

SNAPSHOT SUMMARY

This chapter explores the positive side of human weakness.

REFLECTION / DISCUSSION QUESTIONS

1. List and reflect on / discuss common weaknesses that people tend to hide.

2. In your own words, give a summary of what Paul says in 2 Corinthians 12:1-10.

3. Give examples of how Paul was a very normal person.

4. Why do you think God gave Paul a thorn in the flesh?

5. Why do you think Paul never names his thorn in the flesh? What might it have been?

6. Reflect on / discuss why Paul counts his weakness as a blessing.

7. What does God want us to do with our weaknesses?

8. How and why can our most important possession be a weakness?

9. Is it good or bad to have regrets? Explain your answer.

10. How has reading this chapter helped you in dealing with weakness?

ACTIVITIES

As a group: Reflect on / discuss how weakness keeps us close to God. Share some personal stories that may illustrate this.

At home: Display in your home some reminder or symbol of one of your weaknesses that makes you a better person. Think about a weakness this week.

Prayer: Dear God, thank you for weaknesses that bring us closer to you. Help us to look at weakness through new eyes. Grant us the ability to deal with our regrets and weaknesses in a constructive manner so that we may serve you and others to your glory. Amen.

CHAPTER 12
The View from Mount Nebo
(And Then, There Is Heaven)

SNAPSHOT SUMMARY

This chapter looks at God's grace when the doors are closed to a promised land.

REFLECTION / DISCUSSION QUESTIONS

1. What does Mount Nebo represent to us today?
2. List and discuss some consequences that people can't change and must live with.
3. In what ways was Moses very human?
4. Reflect on / discuss how Moses was an extraordinary human being. List some of his accomplishments.
5. What was Moses' sin that kept him from entering into the promised land? Why did he commit that sin?
6. Reflect on / discuss the challenges Moses faced with the people he led.
7. Give some examples of how doors permanently get closed to us.
8. How does it feel to have a door closed to a promised land?
9. How does God want us to deal with closed doors in life, with consequences we cannot change?
10. Why do you believe there is a heaven?

ACTIVITIES

As a group: Reflect on / discuss how reading this book and conversations you may have had about it have helped you.

At home: Share with someone something that you learned from reading this book.

Prayer: Dear God, we thank you that you can open doors for us and that you offer us your grace to face our trials. Help us walk with you in faith on our journey through this life, and help us also to look for the good and the positive wherever we may go. Thank you for the company of others who share this journey with us, and may we remember that you love us and are always near. Amen.